Rock Classics

Yes

90125

Stephen Lambe

SONICBOND PUBLISHING
sonicbondpublishing.com

Sonicbond Publishing Limited
www.sonicbondpublishing.co.uk
Email: info@sonicbondpublishing.co.uk

First Published in the United Kingdom 2024
First Published in the United States 2024

British Library Cataloguing in Publication Data:
A Catalogue record for this book is available from the British Library

ISBN 978-1-78952-329-4

Typeset in ITC Garamond Std & ITC Avant Garde Gothic
Printed and bound in England

Graphic design and typesetting: Full Moon Media

Follow us on social media:
Twitter: https://twitter.com/SonicbondP
Instagram: www.instagram.com/sonicbondpublishing_/
Facebook: www.facebook.com/SonicbondPublishing/

Linktree QR code:

Dedication

This book is dedicated to the memory of rock's greatest rhythm section – Chris Squire and Alan White.

Acknowledgements

This book grew out of a cover piece I wrote that appeared in *Prog* Magazine in November 2023. I'd like to thank Jerry Ewing for asking me to write it. His leap of faith in me is much appreciated.

I'd also like to thank the Yes alumni that I interviewed for that article (or for other reasons) for their time and kindness: Jon Anderson, Trevor Rabin (twice), Billy Sherwood and Phil Carson. I'd particularly like to thank Tony Kaye for going above and beyond to find time to talk to me about this period quite late in the writing process during May 2024. All of these gentlemen were a delight to talk to.

Thanks also to Kevin Mulryne and Mark Anthony K of the *Yes Music Podcast* for their deep dives into a couple of aspects of the *90125* story, which I have stolen from mercilessly for this book and Doug Curran for important bits of information along the way. Thank you also to Peter Woolliscroft for some vital information about 1980s samplers.

Thanks to Julian Stockton and Billy James for their PR assistance on both sides of the pond.

Finally, many thanks to Dave Watkinson for his encouragement, knowledge, memories and photos.

Foreword

It was simple in the 1970s.

When Yes created their best-known progressive rock albums between 1969 and 1978, their method was relatively simple. A process of writing – often on the road – led to a further period of rehearsal and arrangement, followed by recording. Simple.

Of course, it was never quite as easy as that, as those who witnessed the arguments between Bill Bruford and Chris Squire in Advision Studios circa 1972 will attest. Yes never did things in a straightforward way, but the point is that for them – and hundreds of other bands across that decade – the process – the recording and touring cycle itself – was straightforward. Bands went on the road, then they recorded and released another album, and then they went back on tour again. Whether they had the capacity to fill arenas or clubs, that was what they did. It's what everyone did.

By the end of the 1970s, the pressure for hits was on. Recently, I looked at the sales of albums that we considered best-sellers in the 1970s compared to their equivalents in the 1980s. *Close To The Edge* – the album that made Yes an arena band in the USA – is a platinum album in the USA, which means it's sold a million copies over time. *Let It Bleed* by The Rolling Stones (the subject of the first book in this very series) is now double platinum with sales of over two million. Pretty good, right?

However, Michael Jackson's *Thriller*, the best-selling album of the 1980s released in 1982, is 34 times platinum. Album sales were at their height in the 1980s for bands and artists that were at the top of the tree. But for those that had been nurtured with a view to long-term sales in the 1970s, the pressure was on. Sell albums and singles on a much greater scale or perish. Once again, this process was a relatively simple one, and the choices those bands had were stark. Adapt or die.

This book is about the album that took Yes closer to the *Thriller* stratosphere. It spawned a number-one hit single in the US. Yet, when it comes to the bestselling albums of the 1980s, it doesn't even make it into the top 100.

Nonetheless, this was the album that threw the usual tour-album-tour process out of the window. In some respects, it's one of the most contrived recordings of all time. No album that was created in this way should have been as good or as successful as it was. Yet, somehow, it succeeded, becoming the band's biggest-selling album of all time by some considerable margin.

This is how it happened ...

Authors Note

Human beings have a great capacity to skew facts in their favour. This does not necessarily mean that they are lying as such. It simply means that their view of any given situation is seen from their own perspective. As with any story, not every narrator in this one is completely reliable and just occasionally, the information is completely contradictory, meaning that one or more correspondents are misremembering (if we are being kind). In those situations, I have pointed out where the contradiction arises and given all points of view so that readers can make up their own minds.

It is also a natural assumption amongst music fans that musicians are in control and – especially amongst major rock bands – that record label interest is a given. With Cinema and even when the band renamed itself Yes, this was not the case. Atlantic stalwart Phil Carson and, to a lesser extent, the band's manager at the time, Tony Dimitriades, are vital players in this story. The band – then called Cinema – that recorded the initial version of the *90125* album did NOT have a record contract. Phil Carson, it's true, was working on the assumption that they would be resigned by Atlantic eventually, but imagine the pressure on Carson as he bankrolled the band for months, including the cost of recording, without any firm knowledge that he'd see any return on that investment.

This book includes a lot of the material from the piece about *90125* that I wrote for *Prog* magazine in the autumn of 2023, plus sections from my two other pieces about Yes in the same magazine: my interview with Trevor Rabin in the autumn of 2023 and a piece about the *Talk* album in summer 2024. It also includes a few bits and pieces from my other book on the same period, *Yes In The 1980s.*

Unless stated otherwise, any quotes from Jon Anderson, Trevor Rabin, Tony Kaye, Phil Carson and Billy Sherwood are drawn directly from conversations with the author. Comments from Trevor Horn are largely taken from his superb autobiography *Adventures In Modern Recording* but are attributed throughout, and I have also drawn extensively from interviews in the *Yes Classic Artists* documentary.

Yes
90125

Contents

Introduction – The Story So Far

The chances are that if you are reading this book, you have a reasonable grounding in Yes' history in the 1970s.

In some ways, the story of the band is similar to many others. Like a multitude of groups formed in the mid to late 1960s, the fledgeling band – all of whom had served apprentices in other groups except for their youthful drummer Bill Bruford – began to experiment with the form and structure of rock music. To begin with, this was via cover versions and then their own material, led by (then kindred spirits) Jon Anderson and Chris Squire.

Signed to Atlantic, the first two albums – *Yes* and *Time And A Word* showed promise without enticing the record-buying public to part with their cash in any great quantity. Most crucially, they failed in the US, which led to the band being dropped until they were saved by their great champion Phil Carson – a man who will return to our story shortly.

The band were given one more album to prove themselves, and with Steve Howe replacing Peter Banks, they, at last, found some success both in the UK and the USA with *The Yes Album,* a much-loved record by fans and the band alike, with its well-honed progressive rock structures and pristine production. The band gained its first foothold in the US in 1971, and with the flamboyant session man Rick Wakeman replacing the talented but conservative (or at least that's how he was perceived) Tony Kaye (again, more of him shortly), the band's star began a sharp rise. The next two albums – *Fragile* and *Close To The Edge* – saw the band at their commercial peak in the 1970s. Boosted by hard touring and an unlikely US hit in 'Roundabout', the band surfed on the wave of male-orientated rock bands making it big during the era and making huge amounts of money: Led Zeppelin, Deep Purple, Jethro Tull and ELP were just some of the British bands making a killing in the arenas across North America. If *Fragile* represents the band's commercial peak at the time, *Close To The Edge* is probably their artistic one. So much so that Bruford left feeling that the band could do no better, to be replaced by Alan White. Bruford may well have been right.

And then they went and spoilt it all by creating something stupid like … *Tales From Topographic Oceans.*

I jest, of course, but the double album *Tales* – still splitting the audience amongst Yes fans to this day – marked the band's first clash between ambition and commerciality. Progressive rock and the zeitgeist were, arguably, as one from 1971 to 1975, but *Tales* had even diehards scratching their heads.

The straight-talking, straight-drinking Wakeman left after a tour that saw audiences mystified and enraptured in equal measure, to be replaced by Swiss wizard Patrick Moraz and a return to the *Close To The Edge* format for the challenging *Relayer*. The band's sales had dipped a touch by this point, but they were still doing great business as a live outfit, especially in the lucrative North American market, so that's where they stayed, pretty much, before convening at the end of 1976 in Switzerland (for tax reasons, naturally, it's what everyone did in those days) to record *Going For The One*. This saw Moraz suffer the indignity of being ousted in his home country to be replaced by Wakeman. Some might argue that he was manoeuvred back by Yes manager Brian Lane due to the Caped Crusader's faltering solo career. It was a triumphant return and tour, even if sales remained lower than five years previously, despite a shock UK top ten single with 'Wonderous Stories'.

Tormato saw the band reacting to cultural change and a record company that was after more accessible material and hit singles. They got the former and not the latter, although the tour was a huge success, and the album did better in the US on the back of it. However, the band were about to implode, and relations faltered – both in terms of artistic merit and financial imbalances – as they attempted to record an album in Paris at the end of 1979.

This was something of a disaster since the record company were expecting a hit record and had a summer tour in the US booked to promote it. With Wakeman and Jon Anderson AWOL, something needed to be done.

It all seemed too good – too neat – to be true. The Buggles (Trevor Horn and Geoff Downes) were a vocalist singing in a higher register and a keyboard player. They had hitmaker pedigree and Brian Lane – the same manager as Yes. This was Kismet, surely? It seemed so at first, with the band recording the excellent *Drama* in a whirlwind of activity while hardcore fans gnashed their teeth in frustration at the loss of their heroes Anderson and Wakeman.

Horn struggled on the tour, traumatised both by fan reaction and his inability to sing Anderson's parts unless his voice was fresh, which he rarely was, especially in the UK. Once again, something needed to be done.

… which brings us nearly to the start of our story proper as 1981 dawned bright and extremely snowy. Carson, Horn, and Kaye – they may have been bit players so far, but we will speak more of them very soon.

1981. No Yes

In January 1981, with the *Drama* tour at an end, Yes met at Steve Howe's house in Hampstead. Reports of this meeting vary, couched in diplomacy. Howe suggests that there was a mutual split, with Horn intending to work on the next Buggles album and Squire and White announcing plans to form a bandwith Jimmy Page following the dissolution of Led Zeppelin. In his own autobiography, however, Horn suggests that he was effectively fired. Howe reports that he and Downes were left holding the band's name and had no will to continue. Manager Brian Lane, who took some of the blame for the band's most recent issues, lost Yes, and Yes lost their contract with Atlantic by default. Lane would hang around as defacto manager of the band members except Horn, for a while at least, and would reap the rewards when he managed Asia to worldwide success in 1982. Yes were effectively over as a band and would stay that way for the next two and a half years.

Page was part of the same rock star community as Squire, living in Berkshire, while Squire lived in Virginia Water in Surrey, and had cooked up plans to form a band with Squire following a Christmas party the previous year. Given how early in 1981 the Yes meeting happened, it's highly unlikely that the collaboration with Page – and White's participation – was solidified at that point.

Indeed, in an interview with Squire's friend Dave Lawson by Page biographer Martin Power in his book *No Quarter: The Three Lives Of Jimmy Page*, it is confirmed that following the perceived failure of the *Drama* tour, Squire had lost his mojo for some weeks. 'He'd got into a certain [unrevealed] substance and was only getting up at three in the afternoon', reports Lawson.

Gradually, Lawson, Squire and then White began working up some songs at Squire's house New Pipers, with no specific plan in mind. By February, the (seemingly) casual plan that Squire and Page had formulated the year before developed when Page joined the project, working mainly on songs written by Squire, with some riffs by the guitarist. Indeed, the few months that White and Squire rehearsed with Page as part of XYZ are the stuff of legend. Page was initially enthusiastic, and the trio produced several demos. Within months, however, the relationship began to fall apart, scuppered by both musical and managerial disagreements. Initially, Page had cleaned up his somewhat hedonistic act, shocked by the loss of both Zeppelin drummer John Bonham and Robert Plant's son. But gradually, he began to fall back into old habits. Furthermore, neither

Lane nor Peter Grant, Zeppelin's manager, could agree on any sort of managerial or financial policy, and the relationship fell apart.

While XYZ never recorded an album, it's clear that the two former Yes men had music in mind that was a little more contemporary in tone, even compared to the energetic prog of *Drama*. While some pieces from those rehearsals would wind up on later Yes albums, the Squire song 'Telephone Secrets', which never found a home with Yes, shows a band combining musical chops with commercial aspirations. This would become the template for their new band, Cinema.

At a loose end once more, Squire and White recorded a Christmas single, 'Run With The Fox', released towards the end of 1981, something of an unsung classic in the Yuletide sing-along genre, but entered 1982 at another loose end.

Meanwhile, in the early part of 1981, a boyishly good-looking South African guitarist called Trevor Rabin was also at something at a crossroads. Rabin, who was from a liberal family, had grown up in the Apartheid era. He told the author:

> I was acutely aware of everything that was happening in South Africa. It was a really strange time, but when I was growing up, there was a real effort to make things feel normal, even though there was a huge amount of segregation. These things were especially noticeable because my father was very liberal-leaning and my family was very involved in the anti-Apartheid struggle. My uncle was Sir Sydney Kentridge, who was Nelson Mandela's lawyer and prosecuted on behalf of Steve Biko's family, and one of my first bands was called Freedom's Children. I wrote a political song called 'State Of Fear', which didn't make me very popular, as you might guess. When I first moved to London, I had a call from Peter Gabriel. I thought, 'Oh wow, I didn't think things would happen this quickly.' But, in fact, he wanted to ask about my other uncle, Donald Woods, who wrote the book *Cry Freedom* about his escape from South Africa.

In the same interview, Rabin discussed his musical influences. Although he was no stranger to progressive rock, he came from a different musical background to Steve Howe, and being a generation later, his heroes came from a different tradition to the older guitarist:

> Amongst the white South Africans, American music wasn't very big. We believed that the real rock music came from Britain. For me, my first influences were Led Zeppelin and Cream and I always

looked upon Jimi Hendrix as being English because that's where he first broke as a star. But I was also really into jazz. My Dad was the leader of the Johannesburg Symphony, and because of that background, I could read music before I could read English. But, of course, I was a kid, so I wanted to go off to play rugby. I just wasn't allowed until I'd done an hour's piano practice!

Rabin had originally been in the talented band Rabbitt, who had found fame in their native South Africa, but after two albums, he realised that moving to London might provide a bigger audience for his music. He describes his motivations:

The political situation was a big part of it, but as much as anything, it was because we were a big fish in a small pond – our success was limited to South Africa and Rhodesia [now Zimbabwe]. I wanted to stretch myself and try something else. The band were nervous about that, so I went alone.

Rabin signed to Chrysalis, who reissued his eponymous first solo album, and two others – *Face To Face* and the grittier *Wolf*. The latter, despite session work from the likes of Simon Phillips and Jack Bruce, failed to make much impression, with Rabin perhaps not quite heavy enough to appeal to fans of the nascent New Wave Of British Heavy Metal, despite his obvious talent. Rabin was dropped by Chrysalis, although he still had some irons in the fire, producing albums by hard rock band Wild Horses and Manfred Mann's Earth Band.

Undaunted, Rabin started looking for another solo deal but was soon approached by John Kalodner. Kalodner was the first A&R executive at Geffen Records, the label set up by former Asylum executive David Geffen in 1980. The first album the label released was *The Wanderer* by Donna Summer, but it struck gold (indeed platinum) when *Double Fantasy* by John Lennon and Yoko Ono went stratospheric following Lennon's murder in December 1980. The label was on the hunt for fresh talent and, in particular, looking for promising, if unsung, all-rounders. Rabin fit that bill perfectly, as indeed did another of Kalodner's proteges.

Rabin explains:

Around the same time I was producing Manfred Mann's Earth Band, I met John Kalodner. Geffen had only just started out, and they were in the process of signing people like Elton John and

> Donna Summer. Kalodner asked me if I had any material, and I said I was writing for another album, but Chrysalis had dropped me. Suddenly, I'm in the back of a car with David Geffen, signing a development contract. It was quite a shock. My wife and I were settled in Stanmore (in Middlesex, near London), and the next thing we knew, we were in California!

Rabin moved into a house in Los Angeles and has lived in The City Of Angels ever since.

Rabin set out to write new material and produced, during those months in 1981, the bare bones of much that would later appear on *90125*. However, all was not well in the relationship between Rabin and Geffen. Rabin found that he was being encouraged to team up with other musicians with whom he had very little in common and no chemistry. The final straw came when he flew to London to play with Asia (featuring, of course, John Wetton, along with Steve Howe and Geoff Downes).

Rabin wasn't keen:

> I was told that if I didn't do that, I'd be dropped. I decided to give it a go because I was quite friendly with John and Carl. I flew to London apprehensively and we had a few rehearsals, but when I flew back to the US, I told them I wasn't doing it. There's a clip on YouTube of me singing one of the songs that turned up on the first Asia album, and you can tell from the performance that I'm not singing with much zest. So, Ed Rosenblatt, the head of finance at Geffen, called me and nonchalantly told me that I was dropped. I felt a kind of release because I felt possessive about all the material I'd written, and I didn't want it to go to the wrong place.

It was an uncertain time for Rabin. But he has a few other irons in the fire.

> I started sending out demo tapes, and they were rejected. I've still got the letter from Clive Davis at Arista saying that 'while we feel your voice has top 40 appeal, we feel your song ('Owner Of A Lonely Heart') is too left field for the marketplace today'.
>
> There was talk of a band with myself, Keith Emerson, Cozy Powell and Jack Bruce [this would go on to morph into Emerson, Lake and Powell within a couple of years]. I already knew Jack through Cream and because he'd played on my album *Wolf*. I loved

> Keith, too, but that idea didn't move forward for a while. Then, Ron Fair, a fantastic A&R guy at RCA, offered me a deal, so I had the option of that as well.

There was, however, a third possibility. Another executive who had heard Rabin's demos was Phil Carson at Atlantic, who had remained in touch with Squire and White. Indeed, Atlantic had released 'Run With The Fox' by the duo at the end of 1981. Carson felt that Rabin might be a good fit for Squire and White, especially considering their recent sojourn with Jimmy Page. By coincidence, Squire already knew about Rabin, having been given a tape by Yes' former manager Brian Lane. Despite Rabin's undoubted talent, Squire was unimpressed, as he felt – understandably – that the South African was playing music much closer to Foreigner and it might not suit the band at the time. However, Carson made contact with Rabin, who, with several projects under consideration, dithered. Carson, however, put a stop to that, as Rabin remembers:

> In the end, Phil Carson – who's a pretty persuasive guy – called me up and said, 'Come on, stop fucking around', so the next thing I knew, I was in a Sushi restaurant in Shepherd's Bush [in London] with Chris and Alan. We had a play together, and while it didn't sound particularly good, it just felt right.

Squire concurred in the *Yes Classic Artists* documentary, referring to it as 'the worst jam in history' while admitting that some alcohol might have been involved. But, nonetheless, a new band was born.

1982. Cinema

> The thing that was good about *90125* was that you had a new writer in the band who had a completely different sensibility from the band's initial one.
> Trevor Horn, *Yes Classic Artists* Documentary

The trio found themselves in another development deal, financed initially with £150 000 from Atlantic and then by Phil Carson personally, with the freedom to work on material at their own pace at the John Henry rehearsal studio in Islington in London. Carson already had a long history with Yes. As well as rescuing the band in 1970, he'd also introduced Yes to long-time engineer Eddie Offord and had stayed in close touch with the band, especially Chris Squire, throughout their success in the 1970s.

It should be stressed that, at this point, the band had no record deal of any sort. Of course, Carson had hopes that the band would be signed by Atlantic, but at this stage, he was taking a huge leap of faith. If the band didn't work, he was in trouble.

The group needed a keyboard player, and both Carson and Squire saw the logic of bringing in Tony Kaye, the band's original keysman. Indeed, Rick Wakeman was more than mentioned in despatches, but given what had transpired at the end of 1979 and the start of 1980, his participation was thought both unlikely and unwanted. Ironically, Wakeman was going through another bad patch in his career around this time and might well have been interested, which is another rabbit hole for Yes fans to wander down. After all, Wakeman almost ended up in Asia at one point!

Carson confirms that even at this early stage, it was in his mind that Yes should be revived while the band rehearsed in this new incarnation. 'Part of my job is being a marketing guy. A new band is difficult to sell. An established one is much easier', acknowledges Carson. So, having Kaye in the band would take the lineup closer to being Yes from day one. As a bonus, Kaye had a certain charisma and the way he played would also suit the new band. Squire, however, had the job of selling the idea to Rabin. 'Chris suggested Tony', Rabin says. 'I didn't know him, but Chris said that he was a 'meat and potato' keyboard player, a real Hammond guy. He said to me: 'I think he'll be right for the band because you're a little fancy!'

At this time, Kaye was in Los Angeles, running a company that sold rock T-shirts and playing keyboards with Badfinger. The Welsh band that had been signed to The Beatles' Apple label were still striving for success more than ten years on. Badfinger were recording their new album towards the end of 1980 in Miami. It just happened that the place they were staying at in Key Biscayne was next door to a house occupied by Nikki Squire, Chris' wife, and their daughters, so the connection with the Squire family became close. Despite what had happened to him in 1971, he had remained friends with Chris Squire and bore no animosity towards his old bandmate.

Squire and Kaye began to discuss the possibility of being in a band together again, and when Squire and White met up with Trevor Rabin in London, Squire suggested that Kaye and Rabin get together in Los Angeles at Rabin's home in Topanga Canyon. The two got along famously and, in the end, flew to London together.

They called the new band Cinema and started to rehearse material that both Rabin and Squire had originated. As rehearsals went on, Kaye also began to contribute. 'We rehearsed some of my songs and there was also a song called 'Open Your Doors', which Chris had written that had Alan on electronic drums', Rabin remembers. 'We also played the song that we use as the intro to 'Owner' live called 'Make It Easy'.

Importantly, despite Carson's master plan, there was no thought amongst any of the members – particularly Rabin – that this would be anything other than a new band. Commercial sensibilities were at the fore in perhaps the same way that they were in Asia, but more than a year behind. Asia's debut album was released in March 1982, just as Cinema rehearsals were beginning to gain traction, so their success was both a challenge and a spur for this new band, particularly given Steve Howe and Geoff Downes's presence in that group.

Despite the chemistry that the four-piece was beginning to establish, there was talk of a fifth member. Rabin remembers:

> During the rehearsal process, Chris mentioned bringing in a singer and suggested Trevor Horn. I was confused. Chris had told me that during the shows, he started at the front of the stage, and by the third song, he was standing beside the drums. So I said, 'what for?' Chris said, 'He could sing, you could sing, I could sing. It might be good'. But I just knew him as a pop producer. He turned up to rehearsals with a guitar. I said, 'Is that a prop, or are you going to use it?' We just didn't hit it off at that point at all. Within 24 hours, I told Chris that it wasn't working for me. I loved working with Chris, Alan and Tony, but I was ready to pack it in and come home. Then, suddenly, Trevor wasn't there, so we carried on with everything going smoothly.

Rabin also remembers that the music was becoming more complex. 'We were having such fun playing together, and we were introducing some interesting time signatures and some exciting chordal left turns into the music'.

It's worth dwelling for a moment on what the band rehearsed during this period. With a relatively large amount of time to play with, the material must have swung in and out of the rehearsal process on a regular basis, and with the instrumental prowess of Squire and White in the band, songs were bound to become rhythmically more complex, as Rabin says. The raw material that Rabin had provided, like 'Changes', for instance, and 'Our Song', began to take on a more complex form as they developed.

At around the middle of the rehearsal period, Jon Dee, who at the time was the editor of *Yes Music Magazine,* visited the band at the rehearsal space with David Watkinson. The two discussed their visit in detail with Kevin Mulryne and Mark Anthony K of the *Yes Music Podcast* in February 2020. It provides a fascinating insight into the progress that the new band had made to that point. Jon Dee explains how the two of them became some of the only people to see the Cinema band play live:

> Chris Squire was the person who invited me down there. I was talking to him and Alan White a lot on the phone at the time. Nigel Luby [the band's sound technician] was a friend who lived quite close to me in Earls Court, so I arranged the date with him. Nigel made us welcome and got us a cup of tea. In fact, I'd just been to Alan White's wedding reception, so in a way, that made things more relaxed. I had the photographs from that, which Alan was keen to see, so that was a nice icebreaker. The guys were playing on a slightly raised platform, and they were very keen for us to walk amongst them. It was quite a strange experience. First of all, it was really loud and the music sounded really powerful and so energetic. It was a Yes fan's ultimate dream.
>
> They started with a song called 'Carry On', followed by 'Make It Easy' and then a really interesting song called 'Open Your Doors', which had Chris on lead vocals. In between each song, Tony Kaye was basically rehearsing the intro to 'Hearts'. It was interesting hearing Tony's keyboard style, with his rhythm-based playing and his great Hammond technique.

Jon then discussed the set that they played in a bit more detail:

> One of the questions that Dave and I had before we went in was how close to Yes will this be? Or will it be more like Asia? I was hoping that there would still be an element of Yes, but when we heard the music, we were reassured. The other question was, what would Trevor Rabin be like? We now know that his technique is very different [to Steve Howe], but at the time, we had no knowledge of how he would fit in. But he was just amazingly powerful. 'Carry On' was amazingly powerful. Tony Kaye had quite a simple set-up; he had an OBX [an early Oberheim analogue polysynth], two Hammonds and an electric piano [actually a Yamaha electric grand, rather than a Rhodes or Wurlitzer].
>
> Then, they went into 'Make It Easy'. I was amazed at how fast he could play, and I remember thinking that if ever these guys played Yes tracks, he'd have no problem playing the Steve Howe parts. I have to say that what we heard in the rehearsal studio was ten times better than the final recorded version.
>
> Finally, the last complete song they played had Chris Squire on lead vocals; the first two songs had been sung by Trevor Rabin. 'Open Your Doors' had Alan White playing Simmons drums for the whole thing. It was really interesting and might have fitted onto *90125*.

These pieces included the epic 'Time', one of the most notorious lost Yes tracks, which has built up a legend of its own. Rabin explains: 'It's on a Reevox somewhere. I think Alan had it. 'Time' was kind of successful, but we never put it on the album. It would have included 'Cinema'.' It would also have included 'Make It Easy' and the demos that still exist imply that the final section of that song, plus a reprise of 'Cinema', would have closed the piece. Very few copies of the demo exist, although those who have heard it suggest that it may not be the lost classic its reputation implies.

But the band rehearsed in total for eight or nine months (on and off), with Carson continuing to bankroll the time at the rehearsal studio. It should be stressed that the band did not rehearse from nine to five, seven days per week. Rabin and Kaye had lives in the US and so went home from time to time, and while they were in London, they lived with Carson initially ('In the same bed!' remembered Kaye). But being in Cinema became their day job, and after a while, they moved into a flat on Church Street in Marylebone, owned by Rabin's old mentor Mutt Lange's wife.

Kaye also reports that 'work in progress' recordings were done – only ever intended as reference points and demos – at Squire's home studio at New Piper's in Virginia Water. These included 'Time' and some other songs that didn't make the final cut for the album, which we will discuss in some detail later.

With the rehearsal period at last starting to draw to a close, the next question was: who was going to produce the Cinema album? Canadian Bob Ezrin, best known for his work with Alice Cooper and with Pink Floyd on *The Wall*, was the favourite for some time, with Queen producer Roy Thomas Baker – who had attempted to produce Yes in Paris in 1979 with disastrous results – and Mutt Lange also in the frame. Indeed, rumours began to reach the music press in August 1982, with the 'as yet unnamed' band planning on releasing an album in January 1983, produced by Ezrin.

As Lange was Rabin's friend and a strong influence, he was definitely who the South African wanted. But Kaye played keyboards towards the end of the sessions for *Pyromania*, which became a massive hit for Def Leppard and was produced by Lange. He confirms that the producer was determined to steer clear of this particular project, although Rabin remembers a long, boozy dinner with all three of the potential producers being courted by the band. The three legends got along famously, but nothing was decided, and the search continued.

In the end, it was Squire's decision to pick Trevor Horn, as he was a known quantity and had worked closely with the band in the past, of course. The rest of the band went along with the decision, although Horn himself wasn't quite so certain. With pop music in the ascendancy, rock was – at that time – very unhip, particularly in the UK. While the New Wave Of British Heavy Metal and even a modest progressive rock revival had had a little commercial traction (Marillion had signed to EMI and were having hit singles), this was somewhat tribal. The big bucks were in pop, and there were the beginnings of an 'anti-rock' backlash, with rock cliches received with positive hostility in many areas of the record industry. This was less the case in the US, although the dinosaurs of yesteryear were still considered passe. And these musicians – now in their mid-30s – were definitely dinosaurs.

Horn had a growing reputation. The second Buggles album, *Adventures In Modern Recording*, had been a sort of sonic manifesto. At the same time, his work with pop duo Dollar and, to a greater degree, ABC (for which he would win Producer Of The Year in February 1983) meant his reputation was growing. By this point, he was recording the incredibly bold *Duck Rock* album with Malcolm

McLaren – a fascinatingly hip album that combined found music with hip hop, rap and even country.

Horn takes up the story in his autobiography:

> I was interested, but Jill was much less keen. In 1985, Live Aid would make rock fashionable again, but at that time, pop was very much in the ascendancy, and thanks to my work with Dollar and ABC, I was at least a tiny part of the reason for that. What's more, Yes had ousted me from the band not two years previously; why would I go back?

But Horn did go back, as we shall see.

1982 Becomes 1983. The Recording Of The Album

90125 was recorded across four London studios until around July 1983. The start date for recording is somewhat vague. All four studios that were used for the main album had some pedigree. Initial sessions were recorded at The Townhouse in Shepherd's Bush as Sarm (owned by his wife Jill Sinclair's Father, David), Horn's regular studio, was unavailable. Sarm (in Aldgate) would later be renamed Sarm East when Horn took on Basing Street Studios in Notting Hill and called it Sarm West. Horn had acquired the studio from Chris Blackwell of Island Records, who had just been about to sell the studio to Richard Branson, who Blackwell disliked intensely. The first session in that studio – with building dust still hanging in the air (much to the band's annoyance) – was for *90125*.

The final studio was George Martin's Air Studios (AIR standing for Associated Independent Recording). Located in Oxford Street, AIR was the most exclusive studio in London, perhaps even more prestigious than Abbey Road in St. John's Wood. It cost a fortune, so the band only recorded there for a short time.

Crucially, technology had moved on. This was no longer the era of analogue synthesisers. Although they were so expensive that only high-end studios could afford them, the Fairlight and the Synclavier were the new tools for the creation of digital sounds, with both offering sampling functions. Created in Sydney, Australia, and named after a hydrofoil that worked the harbour, the key to the Fairlight was the 'Page R' function. This was regarded as the most intuitive and useable sequencer of the day, being screen-based with a light pen. Music notes could be re-drawn, erased and adjusted very easily, whereas the sequencing section on the NED Synclavier (from Vermont in the US) was a programming nightmare.

However, on the model of the day, the Fairlight II only had 8-bit sampling with the famous crunchy 'Orch 5 hit' sample (taken from a 1960s recording of Stravinsky's *Firebird Suite*) in its library, so those wanting better quality would go to the Synclavier. The best of both worlds, therefore, was syncing up both. Eventually, other cheaper samplers came through with the Akai and Emulator EMU III, but in 1983, the mind-numbingly expensive Fairlight and Synclavier machines were king, and Horn had access to both. Horn also had his own Fairlight programmer in Jonathan 'J.J' Jeczalik.

So, recording began in London with Gary Langan as chief engineer. But Horn struggled initially. Having dealt with new technology and relatively pliable artists, he now had to deal with experienced musicians with opinions of their own. They had egos and their own quirks from years of recording. Initially, Horn began to feel that this project was a 'ship beset by turbulence'.

Although their relationship was certainly improving, Horn and Rabin locked horns over the approach to recording Alan White's drums. Robert 'Mutt' Lange was best known for producing AC/DC and Def Leppard with a drum style that Horn felt was wrong for such an expressive player as White. Rabin was given an opportunity to record the drums 'Mutt Style', which didn't work, and the South African graciously accepted defeat.

Recording progressed at the two Sarm studios in London, with a further session at AIR. It was there that the Grammy-winning instrumental 'Cinema' was recorded, and a less successful song called 'Red Light, Green Light' (which was to form the basis of the Art Of Noise song 'Beatbox' when Langan looped Alan White's drum pattern from that recording). 'Cinema' was to open a long track called 'Time', which was never recorded in full for the album. Due to how expensive the studio was, Horn begged Squire, famed for his terrible timekeeping, to arrive on time. He was five hours late. Horn flew into a rage and had to be restrained by the crew.

It's important to reiterate the fact that, at this point, the band had not been signed to anyone. Carson was now financing the entire venture himself. 'Nobody at Atlantic in the US gave a shit', Carson remembers of his mentorship of Cinema. 'They didn't stop me doing it, but they were totally against it'.

But there was more turbulence to come. Horn was growing gradually more dissatisfied with Kaye's performance in the studio, and after a lengthy session trying to record the Hammond solo for 'Hearts', Horn snapped. Recording stopped for a few days while arguments raged, but in the end, the producer got his way, and Kaye returned to the US.

Kaye remains philosophical about that difficult period but mentions that the atmosphere in the studio wasn't great:

> Trevor Horn didn't want me there. He just didn't appreciate my input into the album. Chris was behaving badly, and Trevor wasn't happy with that, so it was a strange, uncomfortable time, to put it mildly, and there was a lot of negativity going down. Horn was

> Chris' choice because of what had happened in the past. By contrast, at one point, I was brought into a Def Leppard session with Mutt Lange, who Trevor Rabin really wanted to produce *90125*.. When I did that session, I realised what a difference there was when you had a producer who was confident and in charge, so I experienced two very different things, and it became obvious to me with Horn that the situation was somewhat strange. Even when we tried to put the drum tracks down at Sarm West, things didn't go well. We were mainly recording at his two studios, so Trevor and his wife were also in control of that, including recording expenses, which were considerable, so there was some tension about that as well.

Meanwhile, Kaye moved back to his previous life in Los Angeles.

> I had to go back anyway at some point because I was committed to a tour with Badfinger, but then Tom Evans died [the Badfinger member took his own life in November 1983], that fell apart and also I had a company that produced rock memorabilia and T-shirts, so I was pretty busy when I got back. For me – at that point – it was all over and I didn't think about it at all. I had no idea if it was going to be successful. I was even at the point of talking to a lawyer, as Phil Carson owed me some money. I was at a Sunday afternoon swap meet selling T-shirts when this song ['Owner' of course] came on the radio. Of course, I knew the song, but I'd never heard 'Owner' in its full form. It was on the radio every ten minutes. I knew it was going to be a number one and it was. It wasn't long after that that I got a call from Trevor Rabin asking me to come on tour with the band.

But in the meantime, Rabin, who remained loyal to Kaye but who had also shown his considerable prowess when he suggested a part for 'Changes' to Horn, was then enlisted to play most of the keyboards on the album. Horn has asserted that he was not trying to fire Kaye from the band, just the *90125* sessions, but understandably, Kaye took it hard at the time.

Kaye places the timing of all this quite late on, suggesting he left very close to the time that Anderson was approached to return.

> I was there for most of the recording, except 'Owner Of A Lonely Heart' and 'Leave It', which were recorded very late in the process, after I'd gone. I think Jon came back very soon after I'd left.

He confirms that he was also involved in the sessions at AIR Studios when the band recorded 'Cinema'.

Horn has been at the heart of two major decisions to dispense with keyboard players in Yes history. In 1983 and in 2011, when Geoff Downes replayed Oliver Wakeman during the *Fly From Here* sessions. Does this make Horn difficult to work with or just a driven individual trying to get the best out of any given project? Towards the end of the recording process, in the middle of May 1983, Horn and Squire went to see Canadian rock band Rush at Wembley Arena on their *Signals* tour. The band were looking for a new producer, having come to the end of the road with their usual collaborator, Terry Brown. Horn (reports Rush's Geddy Lee in his autobiography *My Effin' Life*) suggested that Lee check with other people that had worked with Horn before committing, the implication being that Trevor felt he was hard to work with, though this is Lee's perception – Horn may simply have been suggesting the band do their due diligence. Case not proven.

Meanwhile, 'We had finished the album', Rabin confirms. 'All the overdubs were done'. Jon Dee even told the *Yes Music Podcast* about visiting Horn at his home and hearing a version of the album without Anderson on it. However, with Carson still financing everything, the idea of getting Jon Anderson back into the band began to gain traction, with Horn and Carson in favour, while Squire and White were resistant – although Carson insisted that the band were a much better commercial prospect with Anderson on board. Feelers went out, and an approach was formulated. Carson, who had always had a good relationship with Anderson, was the first to make contact but didn't have a current number for the vocalist. 'I got hold of Jon's roadie, who said that Anderson was in a call box on the King's Road in Chelsea waiting for a call from him right there and then. He gave me the number and I called Jon instead. Even though there had been a lot of bad blood, Jon expressed interest but demanded that Chris call him'. Squire took some persuading but agreed.

Anderson was in London visiting family. 'Chris called me and wanted me to hear some of the music he'd been making.' Anderson told the author. 'We sat in Chris' Bentley and he played me some of the songs. It was clear that Trevor Rabin could play, and I was impressed that Trevor Horn was on board as I'd liked *Duck Rock*, the album he'd done with Malcolm McLaren. Chris played me 'Owner' and asked me if I'd like to come in the day after to sing it and work on the verses, as they hadn't got them together at that point'. Anderson came to the studio to sing the track. 'I Told Chris that it sounded a bit like Yes. To which Chris said, 'That's why you're here''. After a difficult meeting with Horn, given that Horn had replaced him as Yes' singer, Anderson came on board. 'I spent two or three weeks working on the album, adding bits here and there, especially on 'Hearts', which I really like', Anderson confirms.

Rabin still has a strong vocal presence on the album, especially on 'Owner', 'Changes' and 'Leave It'. Squire is showcased on the song he originated, 'It Can Happen', and also on 'Changes', where his harmony vocals with Anderson on the song's chorus are enough to melt any old Yes fan's heart. Anderson says that Rabin's vocal role 'was mainly diplomatic' since Rabin had written so much of the material. But Rabin was initially shocked to have Anderson involved. 'To rephrase what you're saying, you want to fire me as the singer', he remembers saying. 'I meant it semi-tongue in cheek. I've never been too proud or jealous about being the singer'. Ever the pragmatist, he saw the sense in handing the vocals over to Anderson.

Anderson and engineer Langan did not see eye to eye and took an instant dislike to each other. Horn reports that the engineer became increasingly exasperated with the vocalist and switched off the automatic talkback button in the control room. So, when Anderson said something like 'spool to the middle eight', Langan would press down the button to say 'Ok, Jon' and then would lift his finger off so that Anderson couldn't hear his addition of '... you twat'. Horn advised Langan not to do that in case he got it wrong, but thankfully, he never did. Horn and Anderson locked horns occasionally, but reports that they clashed badly seem to have been exaggerated. Many Rabin lead vocals were left in place through a mixture of diplomacy on Anderson's part, convenience and creative choices.

Carson was still desperate to get Atlantic fully on board, and with Anderson in the band and 'Owner' in the can, he was ready to play the track to label boss Ahmet Ertegan. It was not as easy as he had hoped. 'Fortunately, Ahmet was visiting Paris. So I grabbed a cassette of the track and sent it over to the Paris office. I told Ahmet that I was going to be on the next plane. So I got to his hotel and all we had to play it on was this tiny cassette player. It wasn't even a boom box; it was a mono player. To make matters worse, the battery was pretty flat. So the tape kept skipping'. But in the end, Ertegan liked what he heard, to Carson's immense relief. 'He believed what I was saying about the band's potential, agreed to sign them and I got all the money I'd invested back, much to the displeasure of the hierarchy at Atlantic US.'

The deal might have been in the bag, but there were still undercurrents of the dissatisfaction that had lingered for months, as Horn confirmed in his autobiography:

> Most of the band were absent when it came to mixing the record. Chris [who still lived in the UK] would join us in the late evening most days, but the others were in America, so it was mainly Gary and me in the darkened control room mucking about with a glove puppet and a ventriloquist dummy that I'd made from a pop shield, called Old Papa Shield. Little tricks to stop us going mad from hearing the same songs repeatedly.
>
> We were using two analogue multitrack tape machines – one 16-track with the backing tracks on it and one 24-track with the vocals and keyboards on it. We spent weeks on it, but I thought we were getting really good results, so I sent the first four mixes to America for the others to hear.

Hearing nothing, and with only 'Hold On' to mix, Horn asked the band's manager, Tony Dimitriades, what was happening, only to be told that they didn't like the mixes, especially (as Horn expected) the drum sound. Horn went mad and almost quit the project there and then. A few stand-offs later, hatchets were buried, and with Rabin back in London, the final mixes were completed in relative harmony.

With this being a new Yes and with not everyone, especially Rabin, completely on board with the idea, a traditional Roger Dean cover was never considered. Artist Gary Mouat, who had already worked with Trevor Horn and who specialised in computer-generated art, was asked to produce a contemporary new cover design. Such a bold image was considered appropriate as his style fitted in with the modern production techniques the band were using sonically. When he created the first artwork, the band were still called Cinema, so the grey Y that is wrapped around the middle ellipse was originally missing its tail and was on its side, creating the C of Cinema. Initially, the album was to have a traditional title, but in keeping with the radical, minimalist tone, the record was simply named after its catalogue number, that being '80102'. However, when it became apparent to Carson that the number was not available across all territories, *90125* became the title. Mouat told Prog magazine in 2015:

> I know some fans think that the sleeve was inappropriate, but Yes wanted something completely different to the Roger Dean works and were interested in using modern design technology as it fitted the new production techniques they were using. As for the album's name, the band were coming up with ideas for names for the album, such as 'Reunion'. One day, I just suggested that they could just use the catalogue number. I've actually still got some rough tour t-shirts and sleeves with the original number on.

Calling the band Yes had more benefits than just commercial ones. With the name Cinema gaining traction, several other bands smelled big bucks and tried to sue, although, as Rabin noted, they never tried to sue each other. For a short while, the band were also to be called Ice. But calling the band Yes was far simpler for everyone – except, perhaps, Rabin.

The album was finished with Anderson now a member of the band, but without Kaye. However, there was one more twist in the tale. With Kaye having left, a keyboard player was needed so that the band could tour. Although Duncan Mackay (who had played in 10cc and The Alan Parsons Project) was considered, Eddie Jobson seemed to be the most likely recruit. US resident Jobson was, by this point, already very experienced, having been a member of UK (with John Wetton and Bill Bruford) and Jethro Tull.

Liking the new album when Rabin played it to him, Jobson agreed to join as a full member and attended the mastering of the album with Rabin. He now takes up the story via a piece from 2007 that appears on *Yesfans.com.* Jobson calls his account an 'abridged' one:

> We got together in a rehearsal room and thrashed through a few tunes, including 'Roundabout' (actually not knowing the song too well, I had to figure out Rick's tricky keyboard parts on the spot – no easy task). But everyone seemed happy, so I returned to the US as a full member of Yes and with a world tour only two or three months away. There was virtually no contact with anyone for several weeks as I learned all the Yes material in my home studio.
>
> The illusion of equal membership soon became apparently false, especially once the filming of the 'Owner Of A Lonely Heart' video took place. Despite my considerable experiences with Roxy,

> Zappa, UK and Tull (a wonderful group of guys who treated me with considerable respect), and with more than 30 albums and a self-managed solo career under my belt, no one was interested in any wisdom I may have been able to impart, on any subject, even on the keyboard rig design which had already been decided upon. But I had made a commitment and I wanted to see it through.
>
> Several weeks later, back in the US, where I continued to work on the considerable Yes repertoire, I did finally receive a phone call from someone – it was the manager who had been given the unceremonious task of informing me that Tony Kaye was re-joining the group and would be sharing keyboard duties with me. No discussion, no conferring – a done deal. And the reason? They needed three original members to put to rest a dispute with Brian Lane (their old manager), Steve Howe and Rick Wakeman regarding the legitimacy of the new band using the 'Yes' name. [There were] no apologies, just take it or leave it, so I hearkened to the words of their own song and chose to 'leave it'.

Looking back at the UK promotion for *90125,* which appeared to coincide with the release of the album at the end of November 1983, it's very clear that Jobson is the keyboard player. He appears in all the promotional photographs, and his rehearsals with the band 'a couple of months ago' – so presumably sometime in the late summer or early autumn – are referred to in glowing terms in an article in *Sounds* by Philip Bell. Anderson reported:

> Eddie and Trevor were doing things without thinking. It was marvellous to watch. Ten years ago, it was very difficult to get hold of two musicians who would do battle on that sort of level.

So, it seems the hierarchy in the band and those almost inevitable managerial and legal issues put paid to the participation of a hugely talented player who might have offered up something different to the band.

Rabin's version of events differs somewhat from Jobson's, suggesting in *Rock Candy* that, in the end, Jobson was never a formal member of the band and that they decided to go with a different style of keyboard player for musical reasons. He claims that the only reason that Jobson appears in the video for 'Owner' is because he had rehearsed with the band the day before. There is no mention of potential legal issues around the usage of the name Yes and also no mention of a possible two-keyboard player setup. It's certainly an interesting reinterpretation of the known facts since we have the evidence that Jobson was featured in the pre-release press coverage.

As for Kaye, he knew nothing of any of these proceedings, telling me, with wry humour:

> I had no idea about the Eddie Jobson thing at all. There was no internet in those days; I don't even think I had a cell phone. So I had no idea. Eddie and I became friends later and talked about it. Eddie is a great guy and a great keyboard player, but he's quirky. You can only have so many quirky people in one band.

But before long, Rabin called Kaye and asked him back. Even though Kaye had never played in the same band as Anderson (or at least hadn't since 1971), Yes were whole again.

Above: A largely leather clad Yes, pictured in 1984. Left to right: Alan White, Trevor Rabin, Jon Anderson, Tony Kaye, Chris Squire.

Below: To fit in with this new-look band, the cover design for 90125 used computer-generated imagery created by artist Gary Mouat. (*Atco*)

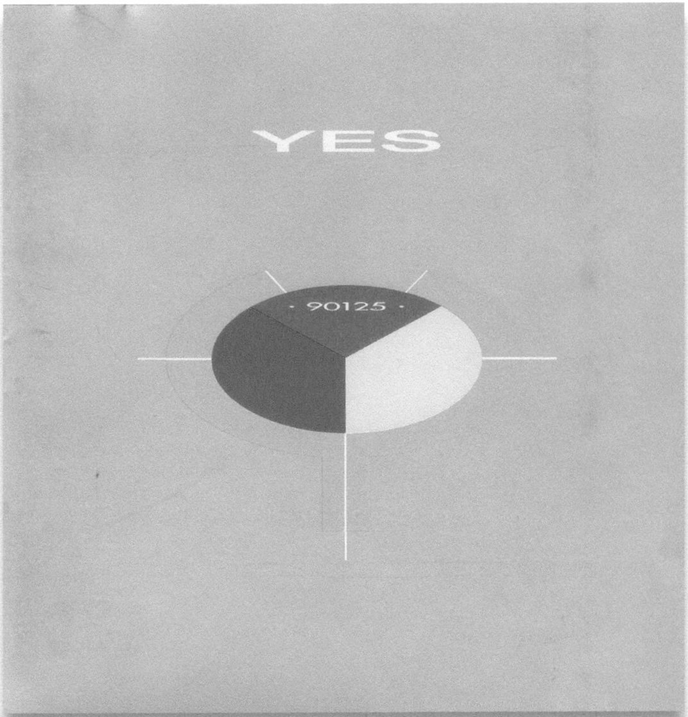

Above: Phil Carson, then with Atlantic, the unsung hero of the Cinema era.

Below: Trevor Horn during the recording of *90125* in 1983. Although his face cannot be seen, it's clearly Chris Squire on the other side of the console. That jumper is hard to miss.

Above and below: Tony Kaye, Trevor Rabin and Alan White during a Cinema rehearsal at John Henry's rehearsal studio in Islington during 1982. (*David Watkinson Collection*)

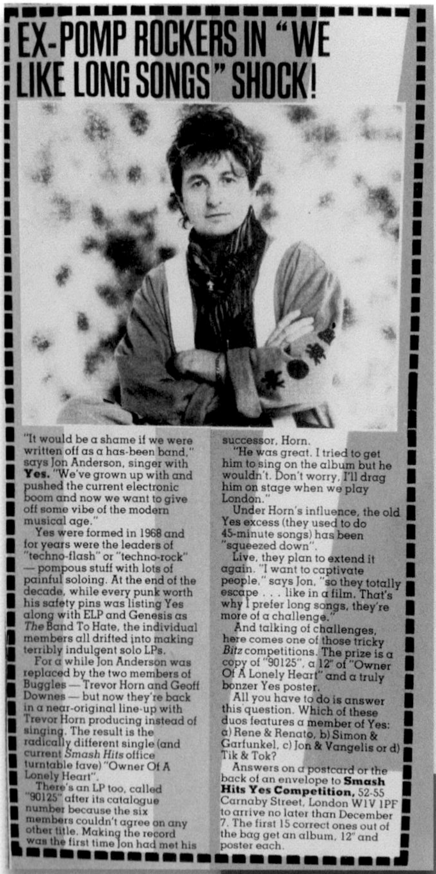

EX-POMP ROCKERS IN "WE LIKE LONG SONGS" SHOCK!

"It would be a shame if we were written off as a has-been band," says Jon Anderson, singer with **Yes.** "We've grown up with and pushed the current electronic boom and now we want to give off some vibe of the modern musical age."

Yes were formed in 1968 and for years were the leaders of "techno-flash" or "techno-rock" — pompous stuff with lots of painful soloing. At the end of the decade, while every punk worth his safety pins was listing Yes along with ELP and Genesis as *The* Band To Hate, the individual members all drifted into making terribly indulgent solo LPs.

For a while Jon Anderson was replaced by the two members of Buggles — Trevor Horn and Geoff Downes — but now they're back in a near-original line-up with Trevor Horn producing instead of singing. The result is the radically different single (and current *Smash Hits* office turntable fave) "Owner Of A Lonely Heart".

There's an LP too, called "90125" after its catalogue number because the six members couldn't agree on any other title. Making the record was the first time Jon had met his successor, Horn.

"He was great. I tried to get him to sing on the album but he wouldn't. Don't worry, I'll drag him on stage when we play London."

Under Horn's influence, the old Yes excess (they used to do 45-minute songs) has been "squeezed down".

Live, they plan to extend it again. "I want to captivate people," says Jon, "so they totally escape . . . like in a film. That's why I prefer long songs, they're more of a challenge."

And talking of challenges, here comes one of those tricky *Bitz* competitions. The prize is a copy of "90125", a 12" of "Owner Of A Lonely Heart" and a truly bonzer Yes poster.

All you have to do is answer this question. Which of these duos features a member of Yes: a) Rene & Renato, b) Simon & Garfunkel, c) Jon & Vangelis or d) Tik & Tok?

Answers on a postcard or the back of an envelope to **Smash Hits Yes Competition,** 52-55 Carnaby Street, London W1V 1PF to arrive no later than December 7. The first 15 correct ones out of the bag get an album, 12" and poster each.

Left: Even the lightweight pop press, with its irreverent attitude towards the 1970s, took an interest in Yes in 1983, as can be seen in this clipping from *Smash Hits*. (*David Watkinson Collection*)

Below: The picture cover for the single of 'Owner Of A Lonely Heart'. (*Atco*)

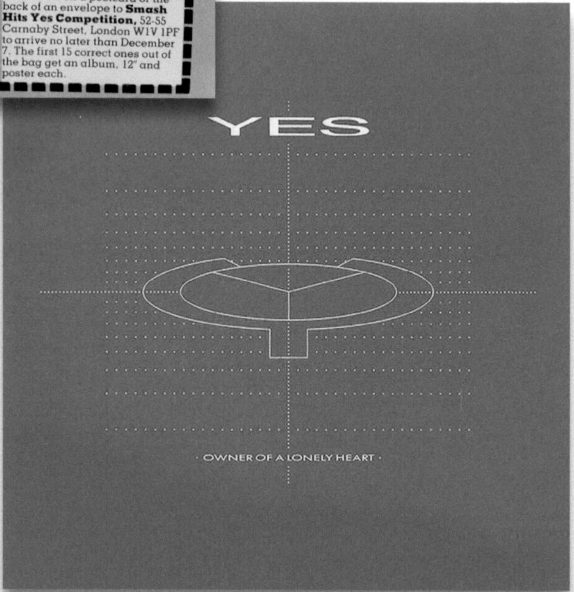

Above and below: Jon Anderson, plus Chris Squire and Trevor Rabin in concert in Dortmund, Germany, during the summer of 1984. (*Alamy*)

Above: A studious Tony Kaye adorns the cover of *Keyboard* magazine during 1984. (*David Watkinson Collection*)

Below: Alan White on the cover of *Modern Drummer* in early 1985. (*David Watkinson Collection*)

Above: *9012Live The Solos*. Something of a folly, designed to accompany the *9012Live* VHS. (*Atco*)

Below: The instrument that helped make 'Owner' such a huge hit. The Fairlight CMI.

The Album. Song By Song

Personnel:
Jon Anderson: vocals
Chris Squire: bass guitars, vocals
Trevor Rabin: guitars, keyboards, vocals
Alan White: drums, percussion, backing vocals, Fairlight CMI
Tony Kaye: keyboards
Trevor Horn: production
Yes: production on 'Hold On'
Gary Langan: engineering
Jonathan Jeczalik: keyboard programming
Dave Lawson: keyboard programming
Bob Ludwig: mastering
Garry Mouat: album sleeve
Released: 7 November 1983
Recorded: winter – summer 1983
Studio SARM and AIR Studios, London
Highest chart places: UK: 16, US: 5
Tracklist: 1. Owner Of A Lonely Heart (Rabin/Anderson/Squire/Horn) 2. Hold On (Rabin/ Anderson/Squire) 3. It Can Happen (Squire/ Anderson/Rabin) 4. Changes (Rabin/Anderson/ White) 5. Cinema (Squire/Rabin/White/ Kaye) 6. Leave It (Squire/Rabin/Horn) 7. Our Song (Anderson/Squire/Rabin/White, Kaye) 8. City Of Love (Rabin/ Anderson) 9. Hearts (Anderson/Squire/Rabin/White/Kaye)

After all those months of rehearsing and recording, *90125* contains just nine tracks. On the vinyl – for which the album was originally sequenced (*Big Generator* was the first Yes album to receive a simultaneous CD release) – there are four tracks on side one and five on side two. While a myriad of remixes and alternative versions of some of these nine songs exist, which will be discussed as we run through the album, no additional songs from the era have yet surfaced outside those that appeared in the *YesYears* box set, released in 1991. As we know, those songs exist, and sooner or later, they will be unearthed.

However, what we do have is a miracle of sequencing. Side one contains just four songs, which couldn't be more different from each other. 1. The big hit 2. The stadium rock powerhouse 3. The quirky pop raga 4. The mid-album AOR/prog epic. Side two opens with 5. The uplifting, Grammy award-winning instrumental 6. The unusual multi-layered pop vocal exercise 7. The 'filler' rock song (although it's not. It's marvellous). 8. The dark, heavy rock song 9. The epic prog closer. Although many Yes fans feel – in some senses, quite rightly – that this Yes was a simpler beast, it's astonishing how varied these songs are when compared with each other. Most AOR bands in this era might bring a little variation into their material but would stick broadly to standard song structures, yet only 'It Can Happen' and 'Our Song' (arguably) have conventional structures, and even these have plenty of variation and quirks.

The point is that every song feels like it is in the right place. The sequencing is perfect. Even 'Our Song', 'buried' in the middle of side two, isn't in reality since it's so different from the songs around it. In a sense, the sequencing almost picked itself.

The Lyrics

Past lyrics on Yes albums were normally written by Jon Anderson, with some contributions from Chris Squire and Steve Howe. The contrived nature of the recording of the *90125* album is matched by the contrived way that the final lyrics were pieced together. The basics of the words were created by Rabin or Chris Squire in the case of 'It Can Happen'. Rabin's lyrics generally express simple sentiments or call up imaginative vignettes. Rabin's heartfelt words for 'Changes', for instance, discuss how he was feeling about life at the time, but can be interpreted by the listener to mean any life change – with a loved one, for instance. In both 'Our Song' and 'Leave It', the concepts of life on the road are discussed, while 'City Of Love' sets a more sordid picture. This is carnal rather than romantic love.

Anderson's embellishments throughout the album generally give a wider scope to each song, however. These are some of the most overtly political of his career. Anderson was clearly interested in the concepts of free will and personal freedom at the time, as we see in a moment. Only on 'Hearts' does he resort to sentimentality found in other areas of his lyric writing, whereas there's a fatalistic warning that strife and conflict can come to us all in Squire's lyrics for 'It Can Happen'.

'Owner Of A Lonely Heart'(Rabin/Anderson/Squire/Horn) (4.30)

UK: 28. US: 1, AUS: 14, NETH: 7

That the band's biggest hit is sequenced first on the album is no coincidence. *90125* was carefully sequenced to work on two sides of vinyl and work it does. Hit them with the big hit straight out of the box. This was not an album just for Yes fans; it was for a brand-new audience. Asia's debut had opened with their big hit 'Heat Of The Moment', and this was Yes using the same sensibility. It's no coincidence.

How the song came to be on the album at all has had some differences of interpretation over the years. It's certainly mainly Rabin's song. He wrote that famous riff and bassline (A BC DD GG) on the toilet and constructed a loose song around it, which can be heard on the first acoustic part of the demo on Rabin's demo album *90125*. Interestingly, the tone of the verses – which had no lyrics at that stage – seem much closer to the final version than Rabin's 1981 demo, recorded in Los Angeles, which has a complete arrangement and lyrics but a much less staccato, more 1980s rock feel.

Horn's story – oft repeated, including in his autobiography – is that he first heard the song during a listening session at Rabin's LA home when the entire (Cinema) band were present. Horn had been unimpressed, but while Rabin had gone to the bathroom, 'Owner' came on the end of the tape. Horn smelled a hit immediately, despite Rabin's protestations that it wasn't for the band. Horn thought that the verse was 'shocking' but that the chorus was 'brilliant'.

However, Rabin refutes the idea that the song wasn't intended for Yes.

> One inaccurate thing that keeps coming up is that 'Owner' was lost in some sort of bad cataloguing on my part. It's not the case. Back when RCA wanted to sign me as a solo artist the year before, that was the song they were really hot on and I knew that it would be a flagship track. Trevor Horn says he had to talk us into doing it, but that's not quite true.

In fact, it was Tony Kaye that heard the song first. When he lived with Rabin at Phil Carson's house at the start of rehearsals in London, he was able to delve into Rabin's repertoire of songs:

> I was the first person to hear 'Owner Of A Lonely Heart'. I told Trevor that it had a great riff and that it could be a hit. Trevor wasn't sure it was right for Yes as it was a pop song he'd been using to try to get a deal. So when we started rehearsing, and the music became proggy, it was pretty much left out of the loop. It wasn't until I left the band towards the end of the recording that it was brought back in.

While the band had not rehearsed the song as Cinema, Rabin says that he always had it in mind, choosing to tackle the other songs with more complex arrangements first. Horn, however, maintains that recording that potential chart-topper was the thing that convinced him to produce the album in the first place. This may – once again – be down to interpretation. It's certain that Rabin knew he had a hit on his hands. Was he holding it back? Did he have some doubt about it being a song for Cinema?

What is certain is that the band did then decide to record the song back in London – but not until they had most of the rest of the album under their belts. When they did start to record it, things didn't go well. First of all, Horn had a terrible time getting the band to focus on the simplicity he was after, with the band used to more complex arrangements. This led to a brief 'we don't think the song is right for the band' mutiny.

The drums were also an issue. The band had never recorded with any sort of click track to make sure they kept in time. Not that a drummer of the talent of Alan White would consider that he needed that, of course. But precision was essential here, so Horn pleaded with the band to allow him to programme the drums with White playing along. Sarm West was available for its first session, complete with building dust. Horn continues in his autobiography:

> The band and I decamped to the newly renovated Sarm West for what would prove to be the studio's first-ever session in its modified form. It was there that I began to work on my grand plan, which was to programme the drums and get Alan white to play over them. We used an Akai MPC 60 for the programming, a great machine that found favour with the hip-hop community.

With Horn, a big fan of the snare sound of Stewart Copeland of The Police, White's snare was tuned to an A in a similar style. White remembered Horn requiring his drumkit being removed piece by piece by roadie Nu Nu Whiting until all that was left was a snare, bass drum and hi-hat. To be fair, White played the part without complaint, but this drum sound did not please everyone, with Whiting commenting that his drums sounded like 'a fucking pea on a barrel'.

The main difference between Horn's vision – for which he deserves a credit even if he didn't rewrite the verses as he claims – is in the boldness of the arrangement, converted from an exuberant rocker into something much more staccato and stylish. Rabin's solo was improvised in the studio and doubled in fifths for an off-kilter tone, while Squire was responsible for the short bridge section, and the arrangement also threw in a crucial key change right at the end of the song – a bold touch.

After his invitation to return, Anderson originally sang Rabin's demo version, but after the verses were rewritten, he was asked to sing it again. Tetchily, Horn reports, Anderson referred to 'Owner' as a 'crap pop song', comparing it unfavourably to Stephen Sondheim's 'Send In The Clowns'. But sing it he did, and it was this version that convinced Ahmet Ertegun to – finally – resign the band to Atlantic. Anderson's lead vocal was clearly a game changer, although Rabin's lead vocal on the chorus was retained. Something that wasn't retained from Rabin's 1981 full demo was his pre-chorus, which was – wisely – ditched completely. It's okay, actually, but it drags the song into AOR territory and sounds like Rabin's solo material.

The lyrics are simple – and considering there isn't a huge amount of song in the first place – reasonably consistent. Rabin's original lyrics comment on its subject's lack of desire to be hurt romantically. The subject wants to sit at home, too scared to take a chance. In the final version, the verses have become much more positive. The subject needs to 'give free will a chance' knowing that he has to 'work to succeed'. This is conservatism (with a small c) and self-determinism writ large. Writer Ayn Rand, who influenced Rush so much, and philosopher Adam Smith would be proud. More importantly, it fits in nicely with the notion of The American Dream. In the UK – where collective action is much more ingrained into the public consciousness – such lyrics might be treated with more suspicion. Is this the reason why the song was such a big hit in the US, not the UK? It might be a small factor.

Anderson's florid 'eagle in the sky' lyric just about works as a metaphor for another creature that relishes individuality, but it's a bit of a stretch. No wonder Horn disliked those changes so much to the extent that we hear a gunshot in the mix after that line, which is Horn and Langan shooting down that bloody eagle.

The choruses return to the defensiveness of Rabin's original lyric by way of an answer to the verses. The character is nonetheless too nervous to 'move himself'. He doesn't want to seize the day, while Anderson's slightly odd half-rap just before the solo is something of a word salad (clearly written by him), in which he advises the subject both not to 'hesitate' and to 'look before you leap'. Which one is it, Jon?

As to the provenance of the lyrics themselves, most are Rabin's with embellishments by Anderson. Horn has very clearly and publicly claimed to have rewritten the verses with Rabin – something which Rabin vociferously denied to the author. That said, Rabin was always very protective of his song. Phil Carson remembers discussing giving away a portion of the song to Anderson:

> I sat down with Trevor Rabin and his lovely wife Shelley, who is very astute. She asked if Trevor would make more money if we did this. I said he would. So, she allowed me to give Jon the credit.

Where Horn (and his team) did come into his own was in the sheer detail of the arrangement. It is possible to hear the isolated instrumentation parts on YouTube, and this throws up no end of detail that might be missed by the causal listener hearing the song on the radio, but which work in their own way to hold the listener's attention throughout the song. 'Owner' is four minutes and 20 seconds long. Let's dive in and look at the song moment by moment:

> *Introduction:* A brief moment of Fairlight percussion (in itself a master stroke – what a confident way to start a song) leads into an overdriven guitar playing the main riff that carries the entire piece. At the end of the first phrase, two snare strikes introduce the repeat of the first guitar phrase, and at the second, there are the snare strokes again, plus a floor tom, and we launch into the full-band riff with the bass playing the same notes as the guitar, and added cowbell. The first phrase ends with those now-infamous Fairlight noises (not just horns, there's an acoustic guitar in the Fairlight as well), and in the second phrase, just before the lead vocal, the overdriven guitar is joined by a second, clear guitar.

> *First Verse:* Anderson comes in on the 26-second mark over the existing instrumentation. The drums are a snare, bass drum and hi-hat. The intervals of decay on each hi-hat strike are exactly the same. This may just be down to Alan White's skill as a drummer, but I suspect sonic manipulation. On 'shake', there's another Fairlight stab – this time just horns.

> *First Chorus:* This is sung by a multi-tracked Rabin (with added Squire) over the existing instrumentation. A little piano motif signals the end of each repeat of the song title. The final 'heart' is extended

with added finger-snaps – a masterful moment of brief tension, released by a whirl of Fairlight harp and more horn stabs, leading at 1.13 to …

Second Verse: The arrangement from the second part of the first verse (though the stab this time is a brief moment of acoustic guitar), but this time, a synth pad adds to the texture before a 'bang' shoots down Anderson's 'eagle in the sky'. There's a brief bass embellishment, another crash and a horn stab before the acoustic guitar stab takes us into …

Second Chorus: As before, until 1.58 (note: less than 2 minutes in, and the main part of the song is done – the last 150 seconds are, arguably, embellishment). The songs open up and become looser in feel. The main guitar line now becomes a fast, clean strum while Anderson vamps over the repeated song title. The bassline changes slightly, allowing a more urgent feel and then there's another moment of tension, leading into a more extensive selection of Fairlight noises, played by Alan White and moving up in pitch, heralding at 2.33 …

The Guitar Solo: Rabin's clever and deceptively difficult solo. It is doubled in 5ths for an odd but appealing tone, jumping around all over the stereo field. Anderson vamps a wordless vocal between phrases. The solo is 30 seconds long – unusually long for a track intended for the singles charts.

The Breakdown: At 3.03, the song breaks down to two minimalist guitar lines and Squire bass swoops before the drums re-enter, leading at 3.18 to …

Third Chorus: As previous choruses, but a slight embellishment by Rabin on the first 'heart', leading into a reiteration of the more urgent version of the chorus at 3.48, with the heavenly synth becoming dominant and a clever key change just before the fade out, which also has Rabin adding a new melody as the song fades away.

In total, the title of the song is sung 19 times.

In the *Yes Classic Artists* documentary, Horn noted White's inspired manipulation of the different sounds of the Fairlight:

> When Alan first played those notes on the Fairlight, everyone fell about laughing. I remember coming in the next morning and saying, 'We've got to get rid of those', and Chris Squire saying, 'No, we've got to keep that'. I'm just amazed at how, if somebody's creative, they can be creative with whatever you give them. I listen back to some of the fun stuff that we did with the drums and I think Alan was amazing.

In the same documentary, Squire commented about how those sounds came to be in the Fairlight in the first place:

> Before Trevor [Horn] produced *90125*, the previous album he did was Soweto [actually *Duck Rock*], a Malcolm McLaren solo album. Malcolm went around all these clubs in New York where they were doing the scratching in the early days of rap with his cassette recorder. He was recording all these sounds and then, of course, they were used on his album, but they were all in the machine, so when we came to do our album, we said, 'let's have a look through Malcolm's library and see what we can use'. In fact, the James Brown horns were one of those samples [those famous horn stabs].

In 2023, the American composer Jon Mattox posted a short video on his TikTok and YouTube channels, specifically discussing the use of cowbell in 'Owner'. The cowbell plays along with the drums – very audibly – in the introduction but becomes melodic as soon as the verse comes in. From playing at a single pitch accompanying the drums, it develops into a melodic pattern in the same key as the song. Later, it becomes more textural, but this was clearly a planned pattern that no listener would hear consciously, but which adds interest subliminally. This is not something the band would have come up with in a million years. It's all down to Horn, Langan and their Fairlight programmer, Jonathan Jeczalik.

There was a final sting in the tail. Unknown to Horn, some members of the band had undone some of his hard work by embellishing 'Owner' in the US. The drums had been changed and Anderson had altered the lead vocal. This seems to have been a move by the US-based musicians (although Anderson was living in France at the time) since Squire was not involved. It was Nikki Squire who alerted Horn to the issue. Fortunately, Ertegun heard the new version, went ballistic and wiser heads prevailed.

There were three different contemporary mixes of the song. 1. The album version (discussed above, 4.29). 2. The single mix (3.53), which fades out before the last 30 seconds of the album version but has no other obvious differences 3. The extended 12" mix (7.04). This bears very little relation to the original song at all, as it was created specifically for the dancefloor. As a listen in its own right, it's largely pointless.

In 1991, when the *YesYears* box set came out, Atco released a 12" single with the original 4.29 version of 'Owner' and three other mixes on it: 2. 'Move Yourself Mix' (4.21), remixed by London-based producer Martyn Phillips. This is a fairly standard remix which presents the album version as recorded, with a shuffling drum pattern, additional bass burble and some extra sound effects. 3. '2 Close To The Edge Mix' (4.45). This first of two mixes by 808 State (who had hits of their own around that time) adds elements from the opening of 'Close To The Edge', especially the synthesised bird sounds, but otherwise seems to do its own thing, mixing in some percussion from 'Owner' and some spoken word from a version the spiritual standard 'Dem Bones', though the performer is unknown. It's odd but strangely mesmerising. 4. 'Not Fragile Mix' (4.07). This second 808 State mix is far more recognisable, mixing up elements from 'Owner' with some throbbing drum and bass and a new – but rather good – synth riff.

'Hold On' (Rabin/ Anderson/Squire) (5.18)

If, on buying the album, die-hard Yes fans were disturbed by 'Owner', their fears were unlikely to be allayed by the track that's up next: the swinging, swaggering stadium rocker 'Hold On'. This was compiled from two different Rabin songs that happened to be in the same tempo (and, indeed, have some similarities in their verses): 'Moving In' and 'Hold On'. The riff and verse melodies were taken from the former and the chorus (with some slight melodic variations) from the latter. I rather like the chorus of 'Moving In'; having said that, it's a shame Rabin never repurposed it.

'Hold On' is big, loud and bold; not in a metallic way, but more in an old-school classic rock style. The verses are sung in harmony by Anderson and Squire (and sound fantastic). It's clear that Anderson rewrote the verse lyrics completely, bringing in his main lyrical theme for the album, which is broadly 'find your own truth in the madness', a much wider and more political subject than Rabin's more personal lyrics, which discussed his own situation circa 1981. Squire has some of his best swooping bass work on the record, and there's an interesting rhythmic quirk in verse two.

The choruses are sung by Rabin and Squire and are clearly unchanged from the Cinema version, although Anderson embellishes with a 'see it through' to remind us he's there. The unusual vocal section – with lyrics probably by Anderson, in which he tells us 'I believe in neutrality' – leads into another iteration of the chorus and another guitar motif before the chorus is repeated several times. This is followed by 'sunshine shine on, shine on through', a moment where Rabin's lyrics – looking towards personal positives in a difficult time – and Anderson's (doing the same thing at a time of global uncertainty) dovetail. There's a big guitar solo to finish. It's stirring stuff.

'It Can Happen' (Squire/Anderson/Rabin) (5.29)
Guest musician: Deepak Khazanchi (sitar, tambura)
Chart places: UK: 92, US: 51
This song was written by Squire on piano and Rabin wrote the sitar-style introduction. It's the one song on *90125* that we know about in some detail since the Cinema version is in the public domain on the *YesYears* box set. Therefore, it's the one track where we can be sure that Anderson's contributions lifted a decent song up a couple of notches. In the Cinema version, Squire sings the verse melody. It's decent enough, but it lacks inspiration. These are replaced by an effects-laden verse sung by Anderson, once again tackling weightier subjects than Squire's more personal lyric. Squire provides the stuttering (but highly effective) backing vocals across some heavily reverbed piano. Squire's bass riff that runs through the intro, with its Eastern effects, is another quirky delight.

Squire's lyrics and melody are retained for the pre-chorus, which is more conventional in tone, with a chugging guitar, although Anderson takes over for the 'It Can Happen' refrain before an Anderson-dominated middle eight leads into the pre-chorus and chorus once again.

The almost unintelligible spoken word section over Rabin's (very good) solo is from *The Importance Of Being Earnest* by Oscar Wilde, and we then go into a section where the refrain is repeated, and Rabin adds some 'la la' vocals. While the first three minutes of the song are full of interest, this is one that actually benefitted from having a minute removed for its single version, which takes out the solo and Oscar Wilde section, good though it is.

British-Indian musician Deepak Khazanchi, best known as part of the Bhangra music group Heera, plays on this track, adding an authentic Eastern flavour, although similar lines are played by Rabin in the earlier version.

'Changes' (Rabin/Anderson/White) (6.20)
From a song that outlives its welcome slightly to a brilliantly crafted, stone-cold Yes classic. Without a doubt, it is in this author's top ten.

If there's one song that sums up the journey that the music for this album went on, it's this. It began as a fairly straightforward Rabin song, with a personal lyric, written at a time of mild depression for the guitarist when his development deal with Geffen was failing. While the subject of his lyric is general enough to be anyone – friend, lover, family member, for instance – it is most likely to be the Geffen organisation itself, who Rabin felt had turned on him. The song then went into the Cinema machine for arrangement, and at some point, White wrote the percussion introduction. He later heard it in a mall and wondered if he should be getting a personal royalty on it. The progressive section after that part is thrilling, as it morphs into a 4/4 section and the song itself begins, sung by Rabin. 'I'm moving through some changes, I'll never be the same', he sings before Anderson and Squire take up the chorus, singing Rabin's lyrics. It's tuneful, powerful and moving, allowing Rabin to riff away with passion. In fact, it's the emotion in the song that makes it – and those emotions belong to Rabin.

That said, one of the great pleasures of this album remains the amount of times we get to hear Anderson and Squire sing together. Although there are some instances on other albums, it's a unique noise that is heard less often on Yes albums than you'd think – it's far more prevalent when the band play live.

The 'one word from you, one word from me' section is all Anderson. Again, he discusses 'liberty', although here, he's more interested in the effect that love has in bringing about change. One suspects Rabin might not be thinking anything as profound as that, but the two sets of lyrics work nicely together.

The piece ends after a final chorus and a reprise of the complex progressive section, closing side one in triumph. It's thrilling stuff.

'Cinema' (Squire/Rabin/White/Kaye) (2.07)
Fading in on a drum roll and a bass drone, this short piece has the feel of an introduction, and indeed, it was originally planned as the

opening section of the legendary 'lost' 20-minute piece 'Time'. Here, it acts as an introduction to the entirely different 'Leave It'. It was recorded at AIR Studios in London, where (despite Squire's lateness) they managed to get a great drum sound. There's a tambourine in the mix that irritates this listener, but aside from that, it's a great piece of work based around a wonderful Rabin guitar melody, aided by a terrific rolling bassline and some triumphant synth. It could almost be 1970s Yes, except for some overdriven feedback howls from Rabin's guitar that places the track squarely in the hard rock era. The piece is also the only one on the album to feature Trevor Horn's voice, the producer adding to the angelic 'ah, ah's towards the end of the piece. It's utterly magnificent and a great showcase for Alan White's virtuosity.

'Leave It' (Rabin/Squire/Horn) (4.13)
Guest Musician: Graham Preskett: violin
Chart places: UK: 56, US: 24,
Initially conceived as an acapella number, this song – the catchy 2nd single from the album – was conceived and created by Rabin and Squire, with Rabin writing the melody and Squire the main bass riff, which is played on a variety of instruments. In the end, they decided to add some basic instrumentation – electronic drums, synth, bass and, later in the song, violin and guitar. However, the astonishing overdubbed vocals are the main selling point here, recorded when they couldn't get a drum sound for the song (probably at Sarm East, then). However, once the vocals had been recorded, the engineer accidentally wiped the time code. Rabin then transferred all the parts into a Synclavier and physically played them back into the song. However, with the results not as good as they had hoped, they then decided to re-record all the vocals from scratch. To stress – the layered vocals were not enhanced mechanically – they were recorded one at a time from scratch.

Rabin takes the first verse and Anderson (who has no writing credit) the second, singing part of it in harmony with Squire. He also embellishes at several points in the song, firstly with a little cod-scat and right at the end, part speaking the opening line. Once again, his contributions enhance an already bold but tuneful piece of music.

The song breaks down at 2:40 into a tense instrumental section, with vocals merely providing 'oooos' before crashing electronic percussion introduces a conventional middle eight sung by Rabin. This is then followed by a return to the jaunty chorus and final embellishments from both lead vocalists.

Despite no input from Anderson whatsoever, the lyrics are somewhat abstract, seemingly warning against the pleasures of the flesh for a band on the road, as spiritual pursuits are favoured over a 'young man's pleasures' via 'Goodbye bad, hello heaven'. Double-syllable words are useful rhythmically when compiling bands of layered vocals, so this may also have been a factor in the lyrical choice here. The song references MacArthur Park – almost certainly not the Jimmy Webb song of the same name, popularised by Richard Harris, Glenn Campbell and Donna Summer – but more a reference to the area in Los Angeles.

The second single after 'Owner', 'Leave It' fared less well, although it did reach 24 in the US charts. In the UK, it reached a lowly 56.

Whereas the single version of 'Owner' might need to be sought out on YouTube, the single edit of 'Leave It' is available on the expanded and remastered version of the album, released in 2004. It's a tight, shorter mix with slightly different instrumental effects and toned-down guitars. The expanded version also shows how the song might have sounded in its originally intended acapella form, and it's rather effective.

Like 'Owner', 'Leave It' was also given a bold remix, this time 'edited' by engineer Stuart Bruce and Chris Squire. At 9.04 (and played at 33 and a third rpm), it's a gruelling listen unless you are in a club. It's called the 'Hello, Goodbye' mix with good reason – this refrain (sung by Anderson) and the keyboard chord sequence are pretty much all that's left from the band's version.

'Our Song' (Squire/Rabin/Horn/Kaye) (4.18)

If you are going to put a weak track on an album, as the old adage (that I've just made up) goes, bury it halfway through side two. This was the fate of 'Our Song'. Seemingly the most 'ordinary' song on the album and played least on the *90125* tour, the song was worked up during the Cinema rehearsals (thus, the credit for all four members), with some late input from Anderson. The good news, however, is that this is by no means filler – it's a little gem.

Beginning with an airy synth motif, bass, guitar and drums break in, in a somewhat off-kilter way, showing a fair degree of playfulness with rhythm and metre as the band throw in bars of 3/4, 4/4 and 2/4 seemingly (to this listener at least) at random. This playfulness continues as the verse starts, sung by Anderson, with further bars of 3/4 and 4/4, held together by some remarkable drumming from Alan White. Only in the lines just before the chorus does the metre resolve to 4/4, and the song takes on a more conventional structure into the chorus. There's a guitar break before the second verse, which shows Rabin's mastery of guitar texture, even in 1983 – this would reach full fruition with *Talk* ten years later. The rhythm part is overdriven; the lead guitar is clean. The keyboard sounds – spacey synth and an airy, synthetic-sounding piano – betray the early 1980s era of the album's recording. Squire's bass is both solid and full of energy and flies free as the introduction is repeated and the song finishes after just over four breathless minutes.

The 'Toledo' referred to in the song is not the town in Spain (sadly) but the city in Ohio, and according to White, this is a reference to a Yes show on the *Going For The One* tour at Toledo Sports Arena on 30 July 1977, at which the temperature rose to 126 degrees F. The song also references 'Rule Britannia', although with no real meaning except that the band – at that time – were 100% British! Aside from that, the song seems to be a tribute to the power of music. A noble sentiment.

'City Of Love' (Rabin/Anderson) (4.52)

From a song that was clearly created by the full band through trial and error in the rehearsal room to one that was crafted largely by Rabin alone. However, Anderson's input cannot be overstated. The song really benefits from the vocalist's 'rock' voice and lyrics, plus his vocal melody – one wonders what Rabin's original version sounded like. Hopefully, we'll get to know that eventually!

Rabin discussed the track with Mike Tiano of *Notes From The Edge* in 2003:

> When we finished the back[ing] track for 'City Of Love', that was a pretty special moment because it was live. There are overdubs, but the essence of the song is live. Everything that was overdubbed on the song was vocal or kind of dressing. When we came into the control room and listened to it and Trevor Horn turned it up – we did it at the Townhouse – we all went, 'Wow!'

Rabin's echoed 'City Of Love' voice intones over a two-note riff, initially played by the bass and then taken up by heavy guitar and drums. This song vies with 'Real Love' from *Talk* as the band's heaviest. It works because the band are aiming at a sleazy tone and succeeding, although, like 'Owner', it hardly feels like Yes, and there's even a touch of reggae in the second half of the verse. Anderson – not for the first time – harmonises with Squire over a staccato synth. The chorus, when it comes, breaks the tension and sounds unchanged from what was probably the Cinema version, with massed vocals from Rabin and Squire and a catchy synth riff. Verse two feels like Anderson had more lyrical input, and in the harmony section, he sings with himself rather than Squire (an interesting moment of arrangement detail). Rabin throws in some vocal variations into the second chorus, and the band throw in a unison heavy rock section before a brief howl of guitar and verse three, with Anderson singing, 'once bitten twice shy, no woman no cry' – a reference to the Bob Marley song. Marley was a big influence on Anderson, as he exemplified when he wrote about the Jamaican on the song 'The Messenger' from *The Ladder* album in 1999. Another unison heavy rock section leads into Rabin's bold feedback-laden solo and a sudden end.

The tone of the piece and the lyrics – which describe, in lurid detail, a place of prostitution and drug selling – were inspired by an accidental trip to Harlem in New York City when he was asked to try out as keyboard player with Foreigner but went to the wrong address. Rabin got lucky and managed to avoid trouble, but the experiences fired his imagination.

The song has featured on every tour undertaken by Rabin-era versions of Yes, where it has usually been greatly extended, allowing Rabin lengthy solo time.

'Hearts' (Anderson/Squire/Rabin/White/Kaye) (7.43)

The obvious closer on *90125*, 'Hearts' is the most obviously 'Yessy' song on the album. How ironic, then, that it should remain – like 'Endless Dream' on *Talk* – this author's least favourite track for many years. A view I've now revised, I might add. It is also the song that clearly has the most 'interference' from Anderson, particularly in terms of lyrics, but his influence in the countermelody in the verses can also be felt.

This was another song with elements written by Rabin during the Geffen period and worked up in rehearsal in Cinema. Kaye wrote the delicate keyboard and percussion riff that starts the song, with Rabin's melody on top of that – 'set your heart sail on the river'. Anderson wrote the countermelody: 'hearing, talking, yes, I love you'. It's interesting that a regular Yes lyrical theme raises its head: the concept of life – in this case, a life with one's chosen partner – being a moving river, first discussed in *Close To The Edge*, but here, initially a product of Rabin's imagination rather than Anderson's. The sentiment of the song is also very Yes-like in that its message is relatively simple. Love – as Anderson often tells us – is the answer and we need to teach this to our children, too (another Anderson lyrical trope). It's clear that apart from the chorus and Rabin's parts of the verse, the lyrics are very much Anderson's. 'Be ready now, be ye circle. Be the central force ye life' – only Anderson would have attempted a lyric like that.

The opening verse is pensive – Anderson begins, followed by Rabin's line, and then they sing in harmony, with Squire joining. White plays a simple beat while Squire's bass doubles the keyboard riff, which repeats throughout this section. A linking instrumental passage heralds the next verse, again sung by Anderson, but with backing vocals now taking on the tone of a Gregorian chant, giving this section something of an ecclesiastical tone. After '… be ready to move', we enter the chorus, Anderson in counterpoint with Rabin and Squire's backing vocals.

A return to the opening lines now introduces a heavy, somewhat conventional (but beautifully played, of course) bluesy guitar solo, Kaye's riff and some powerful drums from White (and just a touch of complexity in the bass part) continuing. For some, this might be a touch too much since, up to now, it's all been very intricate and delicate, but this is a different Yes – one that merges progginess with accessible blues chops. We're back to the chorus, and there would be a case for finishing the song there, but no – we have another section, a thrilling surge of old-school Hammond from Kaye over a heavy rock and synth riff (C and D repeated rhythmically) from Rabin. Anderson, drenched in reverb, now gives us the moment of lyrical doubt – 'who would believe you, wise men do' – and we now have a rocked-up version of the opening riff before a return to the chorus, and a more melodic (but still somewhat shreddy) solo from Rabin. A final coda from Anderson over a simple keyboard backing closes the song and, indeed, the whole album.

For some years, I thought this was the song in which the combination of Anderson's delicacy and extreme romanticism fought head to head with Rabin's hard rock leanings, cancelling each other out. But as the years have gone by and the fandom of Rabin has increased, I've warmed to the contrasts. I still think – had the Rabin that made *Rio* and even *Talk* stepped up to the plate here, as opposed to the one that had just made three heavy rock albums for Chrysalis – he might have handled the guitar textures with more restraint. But 'Hearts' represents a moment in time – it remains a 'showcase' track that has stood the test of time, as well as 'Owner' and 'Changes'.

Contemporary Recordings

As already mentioned in passing, the band – minus Anderson, but with Kaye, of course – recorded some 'work in progress' material at a location called Sunpark Studios, London. It's clear that this is another name for Chris Squire's converted garage studio at New Pipers in Virginia Water, Surrey since the Squire solo section of *9012Live – The Solos* was also mixed there. Tony Kaye also confirmed to the author that some material was recorded there.

The sessions were engineered by Trevor Rabin and Nigel Luby (who is sadly no longer with us); the latter had been engineering the rehearsal sessions in Islington. Two of these pieces appear on the *YesYears* box set. However, the date given for these sessions is January 1981, which – unless I've got the timeline very wrong – is impossible. Rabin had just moved to Los Angeles and Squire and White were just recovering from the end of the *Drama* tour. Indeed, January 1982 is unlikely – so we must be talking about January 1983 (if January is the correct month). These pieces of music are sophisticated, well recorded and sound well-rehearsed. A third piece, 'It's Over', which sounds like it was recorded at the same sessions, appeared on the Rhino reissue of *90125*, released in 2004.

'Make It Easy' (Rabin) (6.11)

Available on the Yesyears box set

Also known in demo form as 'Take It Easy', this was one of the songs brought lock, stock and barrel by Trevor Rabin. The introduction is initially played by Rabin and Kaye in unison before Squire (on bass pedals) and White come in and Rabin plays the main, soaring guitar line so familiar from its place as the live introduction to 'Owner'. Rabin's lead vocals are impassioned but a little strained as he was sometimes on his solo material. There's a nice synth run from Kaye just before the chorus, which is excellent, if very much in Rabin's solo style.

It's not hard to understand why Trevor Horn might have taken against the song. 'I was hurtin' inside but you gave me a second chance', sings Rabin – I can feel Horn wincing at that lyric even now. But there's an exuberance to the chorus, particularly, that will have made it a close-run thing.

The song and arrangement feel finished, and the added proggy touches, of which there are several – especially in the somewhat wild last few seconds – feel like the product of many hours in a rehearsal room. The backing vocals are rudimentary but in place, and while the drum sound isn't especially crisp, it's not hard to imagine that the band thought that this was a shoo-in for the album.

'Make It Easy' was also going to be part of 'Time' and would close that long piece, as suggested in one of Rabin's demos on *90124*.

'It Can Happen' (Cinema Version, written by Squire and Rabin) (6.04)

Available on the Yesyears box set and the Rhino remaster of 90125

This is the version of the song that was rehearsed by the band and put onto tape before recording. It begins in broadly the same way, if without the bells and whistles that the Horn-produced version would have. The layered backing vocals are by Squire alone (by the sounds of them) and there's initially some fairly basic synth and some jaunty piano from Kaye. The verse – a bluesy melody sung by Squire, with a staccato guitar from Rabin – was dispensed with entirely when Anderson returned, but the 'look up, look down, look out, look around' pre-chorus remains before the catchy chorus, which again remained intact on the finished version. There's a good solo from Rabin, but the song doesn't really go anywhere, despite a few final 'yeahs' from Rabin as the song fades out.

'It's Over' (Rabin) (5.41)

Available on the Rhino remaster of 90125

The drum sound confirms that this was most probably recorded in the same sessions as 'Make It Easy'. It begins with a big, Zeppelin-esque riff, followed by a lead guitar fanfare. Rabin again delivers a slightly strained lead vocal, and the lyrics on the verse are – frankly – terrible. Although, the chorus – with its Queen-style backing vocals and pensive organ arpeggios – is somewhat better. But of the songs from these sessions that have been released, it's probably the least impressive, although there's some mobile bass from Squire at the end. After a big major chord to finish, the piece feels like it might be going off in another direction as it fades. Was this another section of 'Time'?

Release, Commercial Performance, Reception And Legacy

A friend of mine who's a producer in LA said that he couldn't believe it when he first heard 'Owner Of A Lonely Heart' on his car radio. He had to pull over to the side of the freeway to listen to it as he couldn't believe the sound we were making.
Chris Squire

Change the guitarist, change the group. This is nothing like what I knew. It was more like Asia than Yes to me, and I wondered if they were trying to be like us. 'Heat Of The Moment' had been successful so this was a new thing for me to get used to: that while Asia existed, Yes existed as well.
Steve Howe

As a 1970s Yes fan, I don't know if I hadn't produced *90125* if I'd have liked it. I'd have liked some of it, but I'd have seen certain parts of it as selling out to some sort of stadium rock ethic that I wouldn't have approved of.
Trevor Horn

['Owner'} was a pop pop song and it didn't mean anything to me; I couldn't care less, it meant nothing. Anyone could have done that. I know that to a lot of the diehard Yes fans, that's not true Yes.
Michael Tait, Yes lighting designer up to 1980

These comments, which all come from the *Yes Classic Artists* documentary, made in 2005, demonstrate how those, even with close associations to the band, felt about the new album and hit single. But the public – and critics – were very much on the side of this new-look band.

Released at the end of October 1983, 'Owner' was expected to be a hit, so an expensive narrative video (albeit one that plays with the traditional 'performance' format for its first few minutes), directed by Storm Thorgerson of Greenback Films, was created in London.

The song went in at 62 for the chart W/E 5 November, where (interestingly) 'Don't Cry' by Steve Howe's Asia had just fallen out of the charts, and 'The Smile Has Left Your Eyes' was on the way up to being a modest hit. The next week, it was at 45, and with *90125* now out, it was at 37 the week after, rising to 27, then 14, then 11. It hit the top ten and number seven on 17 December, then four for two weeks into January 1984, two on 14 January and – finally – it knocked the uninspiring 'Say, Say, Say' by Paul McCartney and Michael Jackson off the number one spot in a top 20 that also included 'Karma Chameleon' by Culture Club, 'Holiday' by Madonna and songs by fellow-dinosaurs Genesis and The Rolling Stones. It spent just two weeks at number one before being usurped by Culture Club, but it was enough.

Meanwhile, just as *Alpha* by Asia was dropping out of the charts, *90125* went in at the start of December at 28, then to 15, 13 and seven, which is where it stood at the year's close. It reached its highest position of five during a time when *Thriller* by Michael Jackson was dominant, as well as *Can't Slow Down* by Lionel Ritchie. It didn't drop out of the top ten until mid-March and was still at 65 at the end of June and at 104 at the end of August (but on the way up!) Although in the lower reaches of the chart by December, the album spent a whole year on the US *Billboard* 200, reaching triple platinum status for three million sales. Quite an achievement for a bunch of has-beens and one dashing young South African.

The success was repeated around the world, although 'Owner' was only a relatively minor number 28 hit in the UK, with the album itself reaching a lowly 16. It did, however, hit Gold status, whereas *Drama*, which reached number two in the UK, only managed Silver (Gold is 100 000 rather than 60 000 sales). By this time in the UK, pop music had a sort of anti-rock ethic and a move away from guitar music. This didn't mean that there was no rock music at all, of course, but it meant that, as a genre, it was somewhat more polarised.

Press reaction was largely good, with even *Rolling Stone,* hardly the band's biggest fans in the past, giving it a cautiously positive review, even if tracks like 'Cinema' and 'Our Song' did suggest the band were 'up to their old tricks.' In fact, it's hard to find a bad review of the album online these days, although it still rankles with a significant minority of the Yes community, for whom the entire Rabin era is dealt with as selling out after the band's purist progressive ethic.

The Ongoing Legacy Of 'Owner'

Many bands have a long and varied history (as Yes do), but in terms of singles (or streaming) success, they have one song that defines them in the minds of the wider population. Marillion have 'Kayleigh', Soft Cell have 'Tainted Love' and Yes have 'Owner Of A Lonely Heart'. The band have had a few hits over the years. An edit of 'Roundabout' was a US hit in 1971 and 'Wonderous Stories' reached number seven in the UK in 1977. 'Leave It' (US) and 'Going For The One' (UK) were both minor follow-up successes. Yet, 'Owner' is the song that everyone remembers. In the UK, this is less because of the success of its 1983 release than Max Graham's euphoric dance reworking in 2005, released on the Ministry Of Sound label, which was a huge hit in clubs but also reached number nine in the main chart.

A glance at any streaming site of your choice throws up a variety of cover versions that have been released over the years. There's the song as an acoustic ballad by James Farrellini, a shimmering electronic ballad by Em Sherman and Sea Saint and a straight, faithful cover by Ninja Sex Party. The current fashion for 'reaction' videos on YouTube – often featuring people of other cultures and ages – throws up a variety of possibilities for both 'Owner' and 'Leave It'. If you are feeling bold, do a search for 'Owner Of A Lonely Heart' on YouTube and see what comes up. You may end up down a rabbit hole for which you won't thank me.

For those more closely associated with the song, its popularity has been hard to escape. Rabin played the song on his 1989 tour in support of his excellent *Can't Look Away* album. Alongside the other 'standard' that he has written – 'State Of Independence' (with Vangelis) – a solo Jon Anderson show would not be complete without some sort of rendition of the song. Horn plays the song live with his band (which includes Lol Crème) and has recorded two versions in recent years. An interesting orchestral version (with vocal by Horn) can be found on *Trevor Horn Reimagines The 80s* (2019) and a rather more laid-back version, nicely sung by 80s pop crooner Rick Astley, was released on Horn's 2023 album *Echoes – Ancient And Modern.* Finally, a version of 'Owner' appears on the Chris Squire tribute album *A Life In Yes,* featuring Dweezil Zappa and sung by Chris' ex-wife Nikki.

'Owner Of A Lonely Heart' – for better or worse – will probably outlive us all.

Other Songs From 90125

None of the other eight songs on the album have had the same resonance as 'Owner' as you might expect. Although 'Leave It' gets some love on YouTube for its layered vocals, it tends to be the proggier songs that get the most love.

Anderson has embraced 'Hearts', recording a lovely version on his wonderful *Change We Must* solo album from 1994 with a full orchestra. If you can find it, there's also a live version recorded with a South American band in Brazil from the year before.

Two Yes tribute albums have decent versions of 'Changes'. The best of the two is from the 1995 Magna Carta label release *Tales From Yesterday*, featuring US progressive/hard rock band Enchant, while *Yesterday And Today,* compiled and recorded by Dave Kerzner and Fernando Perdomo, features lead vocals from Robert Berry (of the band 3 with Keith Emerson) and Billy Sherwood. That same album has a slightly extended 'Cinema' featuring the distinctive lead guitar of Steve Hackett.

The 90125 Videos

Prior to 1983, Yes had never been very good at videos. Of course, promotional films were sometimes a necessity, even prior to the MTV era, which began (with 'Video Killed The Radio Star' by The Buggles, ironically) in 1982. They had appeared on many TV shows all over Europe – and some of that footage is online – and there were the promotional videos they did for various songs from *Time And A Word*. The band got a little bit more serious in the late 1970s, but even then, the video for 'Wonderous Stories' is little more than a hastily assembled live performance. There's a little more artifice in the rudimentary visual effects for 'Don't Kill The Whale', while, by *Drama*, the band opted for a mimicry of the live show for 'Tempus Fugit' and 'Into The Lens'.

'Owner Of A Lonely Heart'

However, with much expected of the lead single, it was deemed appropriate for a high-profile video to be shot. Even in 1983, the peak video-production era was already upon us. Expectations and budgets were high. It was in this environment that Greenback Films were beginning to make inroads. The main creative forces behind the company were well-known to Yes, having – as Hipgnosis – designed two of the band's more controversial album covers in *Going For The One* and *Tormato*. By the time they took on Yes as a visual entity, their best-known video had been for Paul Young's UK number one 'Wherever I Lay My Hat That's My Home', and they had settled into a routine. Aubrey Powell and Storm Thorgerson would write a script, and Storm would direct (the IMDB suggests the other way round, but the arrangement given by the author is confirmed by Martin Powell in his book *Us And Them*).

Part of the ethos of Greenback was that they preferred not to have the artist mime in their videos (or short films), preferring instead a more creative story-based approach. This was certainly the case on 'Owner', with the pair creating a labyrinthine thriller-based storyline. For Yes, the video was shot just after their first (and seemingly only) rehearsal with Eddie Jobson, presumably in the warehouse-type location they use for the first minute and a half of the video, which teases the viewer with what appears to be a standard – if slightly sweaty – performance video showing Rabin smiling as he sings the chorus, and Squire miming uncomfortably. To see this part, find the longer version, which has had a staggering 49 million views online.

Suddenly, we zoom in on Anderson as he suggests that there might be another way of 'doing this' and then … silence! Anderson (a bird), Rabin (a lizard), Squire (a snake) and White (a cat) all have transformation scenes, and the song starts again. Jobson was presumably filmed in this way, too, but his transformation failed to make the cut. Indeed, Jobson appears only twice – briefly punching the air in the live performance footage and from the back in the rooftop scene.

The track restarts and we are plunged into a dystopian drama starring striking British character actor Danny Webb, who is arrested on his way to work. He is then dragged through all kinds of bureaucracy while experiencing horrific images of insects and a bird (including squirming maggots; one wonders what animal was meant to represent Jobson. Was it the spider, the scorpion or the maggots?) before making his escape in what appears to be a foundry, climbing onto a roof where he is cornered by the besuited band. With no other option, he throws himself off the roof. Comically, it's clearly a dummy that falls. He transforms into a bird that soars away. We cut back to a crowd of people again heading to work in London. Webb is amongst them but thinks better and turns back …

What on earth is going on? Does it really matter, though? The story – such as it is – bears no relation to the song. Typically, the Hipgnosis/Greenback creatives weren't really interested in the band at all – it was just about bringing their artistic vision to the world. But the budget is, at least, up there on the screen. There are whole filmic setups that last seconds but must have taken hours to light, block and shoot. In fact, there are some interesting moments, especially when Thorgerson concentrates on close-ups; a mother and her baby, for instance, or an official jerking his head by way of curt instruction to a minion. The use of black and white versus colour is also interesting. The band are always shot in colour, yet the main story is in black and white until the fight and rooftop sequences. But overall, it feels extravagant, pretentious and faintly silly.

There are two versions of this available on YouTube. The most seen is the long cut, which has the full band 'false start', the four band transformations (with Squire in his beloved Bentley) and a full cut, including plenty of 'maggot action'. The second has no band performance and only Anderson transforming before a very similar cut of the main story. A maggot-free version was supposedly cut for the BBC, and there must be a rough cut with Jobson fully featured, which has never seen the light of day.

'Leave It'

If 'Owner' was a big, narrative-based production, then the video for 'Leave It' was quite the opposite. The band's manager, Tony Dimitriades, said at the time that the object was to avoid 'MTV music clip cliches' so that there were 'no women or vintage automobiles or desert sands'. Of course, those obvious tropes (see Duran Duran, for instance) were hardly present in the video for 'Owner', but the sentiment still holds. Of course, cost may also have been an issue. But from one set of auteur video makers in Po and Storm, attention now shifted to another creative duo – Kevin Godley and Lol Crème.

The duo had, of course, been two of four-man pop and rock outfit 10cc before striking out as a duo with that huge, unique folly *Consequences* and a series of less ambitious but always challenging albums. They had cut their teeth on their own video for 'An Englishman In New York' from their *Freeze Frame* album and had gone on to acclaim and, indeed, awards for the bonkers 'Rockit' by Herbie Hancock and the starkly minimalist 'Every Breath You Take' by The Police.

If you are reading this book, there's a good chance you've seen the video for 'Leave It'. The band stand side by side in grey suits, upside down, lip-synching to the song. Dated 1980s special effects whirl them around. It's not very exciting. But that's not the point.

The band filmed the video in New York in one day just before the tour started. 'The basis of this video is one shot,' Crème told MTV at the time, 'with the band intentionally made to look as bland and undemonstrative as possible. Your perception of the video will be altered because it will be upside down'. He's not wrong. The directors initially wanted to hang the band upside down, but much to their relief, the idea was scuppered by Rabin's ongoing recovery from the spleen operation, which had already delayed the tour. Indeed, Rabin's state of health was the source of some amusement, with Rabin seen telling Godley that 'they found I had four spleens'. With one removed, he then became 'the man that has three spleens'.

In a mixture of bold creativity and tongue-in-cheek performance art, the directors shot the band 18 times. Godley and Crème gave each version a bizarre, Python-esque name. Thankfully, MTV were there to video the recording session, and on the poor quality MTV footage, now available on YouTube, some take names are difficult to read, but these are the ones that can be seen:

V1. Basic Charcoal Grey
V3. Tribute To Jeremy

V4. Endless Infatuation
V5. 4
V7. Zoom For Zoom's sake
V8. Surgeon's Dilemma
V9. ????? [this was the actual title]
V10. Lords Of The Galaxy
V14. Here Today Gone Tomorrow

The MTV 'Making of' teases many different versions. One (later revealed as version seven) has just Anderson and nobody else. Another has Rabin jumping up and down. Another has the band replaced by five other people, including Atco vice president Sheldon Vogel as 'Trevor Rabin'. Another has the band replaced by their instruments (in Anderson's case, a mic on a stand), and yet another is a standard version with Tony Kaye wearing a pink tie.

One take, shot late in the day, has the band mime to the entire song with their backs to the camera, during which the directors quietly ushered the crew out, so as soon as the band turned round, the studio was empty save for one cameraman. The band take the joke in good heart – 'I knew it', says Kaye, while someone (probably White) just exclaims, 'You wankers', and Anderson (who first approached Godley and Crème) can be heard giving a single-word response: 'Beautiful'.

Those versions in the can, Godley and Crème then went into an editing suite and created a variety – perhaps (but not necessarily) 18. The point here – somewhat missed by commentators – is that the final versions did not necessarily correspond with the versions shot since they cut various different takes together in some cases. This means that it's possible that some of the 18 versions filmed may well never have been seen outside of the MTV documentary.

Godley and Crème organised a competition inviting MTV viewers to work out what was different about the versions, and 12 cuts were broadcast between 25 and 31 March 1984, with 15 shown back-to-back on 1 April. The prize? A VHS video of every version. So, presumably, there are Yes fans with playable VHS copies out there somewhere. If you are one of them – please get in touch!

With initial promotion at an end and the song a minor hit in the US, the video drifted out of rotation, and version 11 became the standard one, available online and on *Greatest Video Hits*, released in 1992.

As a final aside, label Atco were not consulted about the video at all – the band and Tony Dimitriades presented it to them as a fait accompli, something the label appeared to take in good heart. Indeed, they must have known something about it, or Sheldon Vogel would not have been present at the recording.

'It Can Happen'

Filmed on a day off from touring, the video from the fairly unsuccessful third single is a much more conventional 1980s performance, with the band swirling around the camera. It's functional at best, and the band were not enamoured by the huge amounts of makeup they were required to wear. The name of the director seems to have been lost to the mists of time.

'Owner Of A Lonely Heart' (Alternative Version)

Not sanctioned by *Yesworld.com* but available on YouTube is a second version filmed for German TV, the band performing in a studio desert set, with the budget stretching only to four stuffed parrots. This version seems to have been disowned by everyone, with good reason. It's ghastly, but at least it has Tony Kaye in it.

The 90125 Tour, Video And Live Album

It was inevitable that the band would tour in support of the album, which involved visiting the sort of venues that Yes had traditionally played at in the 1970s – big arenas in the US, with a similar schedule in Europe, planned for the summer of 1984, with another visit to the US later that summer. The audio system was designed by Clair Brothers, the US-based audio company that had worked with the band in the 1970s. Cash was thrown at the visuals, too. Yes were truly back in the big time.

But there were a couple more stings in the tail. The early dates of the tour planned for late January 1984 were postponed when Rabin suffered an unfortunate, if faintly comical, accident. 'My wife and I went to Florida just before the tour and I had an accident in a swimming pool. A woman came down a slide and hit me, which led to my spleen being removed. We'd decided to celebrate as we'd just heard that 'Owner' had gone to number one and that the album was top five. So the tour was delayed.' The suits were not happy.

Rabin took a few weeks to recuperate, which also meant time off from practice.

> In the meantime, I'd barely played the guitar, and I certainly hadn't played any of the older Yes stuff. I had never really wanted to call the band Yes in the first place, so now I was stuck with playing some of the old Yes tunes in what I considered to be a new band. Chris reassured me, 'You choose what you want to play'. On the plane to rehearse in Philadelphia, I came up with some ideas. I was concerned that my guitar style was totally different from Steve Howe's, so Chris also said, 'You do it your way. It'll make the band sound like its own thing'. That made me feel warmer, and it made the tour much easier.

When I discussed the *Talk* tour with Rabin, he revealed that rehearsals were always a problem for the band, which he found frustrating:

> In all the years touring with Yes, we never played through the entire show at rehearsals. It drove me nuts! Tony was always well-prepared, but the first few shows were usually more of a rehearsal.

But with the band in rehearsals in early 1984 and a draft set list finally chosen, Kaye had to reproduce a lot of the studio sounds of *90125* live. He needed a keyboard rig that could supply that.

Enter Casey Young, an award-winning synthesiser player with a growing portfolio of clients and a reputation for creative keyboard rig creation. Young's position below decks came about more for practical reasons than for egotistical ones (Young told the *Yes Music Podcast*) since the stage set – stark and sleek in the 1980s style, with no amps or other extraneous (by 1980s standards) equipment on stage – had already been designed by this point. Much later in the tour, when the band played open-air shows on other people's stages, Young played on the same level as the band, if somewhat apart.

He explained what his initial role was to be for the *90125* tour and how it expanded on the *Yes Music Podcast* in 2020:

> I got a call in 1983 from Tim Myer, a guitar tech deluxe for many bands, and he knew my keyboard design chops and my synthesiser programming. He asked me to design a system for Tony Kaye and to reproduce the sounds on that record [*90125*]. So, they hired me to put that rig together, which was a really fancy rig for 1983. If you remember, midi [a digital system that allows instruments to talk to each other, still very much in use today] was just coming in, but it wasn't implemented on everything, so we had our work cut out. They asked me to programme it, and then I went back for rehearsals to get Tony going on it. About halfway through rehearsals at Clair Brothers [who were providing Yes' sound system for the tour], they wanted Tony to add another sound to the song 'Hearts', and Tony said, 'I'm full up, all my presets are loaded, I can't do it.' Chris looked at me and said, 'He can'. I said, 'I can't go – I've got sessions to do!' So, we talked about it, and finally, Jon said to me, 'Run away with the circus; give it a try for a couple of days, see if you like it.' Two years later, I was still playing with the band.

Tony Kaye is protective of his role at this time and gives a rather more blunt description of Young's role in the band. 'He was my keyboard tech.' He says. It's understandable. Kaye has been the victim of a conspiracy theory over the years – ridiculous, of course – that he was miming throughout the tour and that Young was actually the keyboard player from below the stage. This is ludicrous for a variety of reasons, particularly as Kaye was clearly a better and more experienced player than Young. The American's expertise was in rig design, not in virtuosity. Technology, not technique, as it were. Secondly, every bit of footage of the tour demonstrates that Kaye is playing, and finally, while extra musicians are often featured onstage (as Billy Sherwood was during the *Talk* tour in 1994), at this time, they often weren't, especially (though far from exclusively) keyboard players in heavy rock bands.

What Young actually played developed over time. Initially, he was mainly triggering vocal enhancements, such as on 'Changes', but when Anderson suggested he acquire a vocoder (a keyboard device that processes vocal lines, as first used by Yes on the *Drama* album), he (he claims) had parts thrown at him constantly. Anderson sometimes asked him to play new parts with minutes notice and he often had to double Rabin's guitar lines, which took some concentration. Young was grateful not to have to 'perform' as the other musicians were required to. Indeed, while for most of the band, playing these shows was in their DNA, for Rabin, it was something of a culture shock that saw him overcompensating early on in the tour. 'After the first gig, I remember Nu-Nu Whiting saying that I should have a satchel [in Angus Young style] as I'd been jumping around so much. So I calmed down a bit after that.'

The setlist for the tour remained fairly static, but songs moved around somewhat and the terrific 'Our Song' wandered in and out of the set. But the rest of the album was featured in a well-balanced show. Proceedings began with 'Cinema' segueing into 'Leave It' (with White playing electronic drums), followed by the more bombastic 'Hold On'. Initially played towards the end of the set, the dynamic 'Hearts' was later switched to the first half, with the show-stopping 'Changes' played mid-way through. 'Owner' and 'It Can Happen' were generally performed late on, with an extended 'City Of Love' often closing the main set, although 'Starship Trooper' was sometimes played before the inevitable encore of 'Roundabout'. The older material was mainly taken from 1971's *The Yes album*. This made sense since they were the pieces that Kaye had last played on with Yes, but were also the songs that best suited Rabin, who has always professed a love for 'Perpetual Change' in particular. Only 'And You And I' and the encore represented other areas of the band beyond Anderson and Squire's solo sections.

The initial leg of the tour took in the US and Canada from February to May 1984, and after a few weeks break, the band reconvened in Europe for the Summer, arriving in the UK in July. A further two-month jaunt around the US and Canada up to October was followed by the first Rock In Rio at the purpose-built Citade Do Rock in Rio de Janeiro early in 1985. Almost 1.4 million people attended this ten-day festival, which saw Yes, Queen, George Benson, Rod Stewart and AC/DC each headline two nights. After further dates in Uruguay and Argentina, the *90125* tour officially came to an end in February, a year after it had started.

9012 Live Video, DVD and Live Album

A little more than one hour of a live show in September 1984, filmed in Edmonton, Canada, was released on VHS in 1985 and later on DVD in 2006, with additional backstage footage, called *Access All Areas*. The film was directed by a young Steven Soderbergh, who would go on to fame with his indie debut *Sex, Lies And Videotape* in 1989, and a career that also included the 'Ocean' series starring George Clooney. As well as capturing some excellent concert footage, Soderbergh mixed in footage from a short film called *Young Man's Fancy* from 1952 (effectively an infomercial for Edison Electrics), plus an array of dizzying video effects – that have dated very badly indeed – designed by a company called Charlex. Other dated aspects include the stage clothes – very much 'of their time' – and the stage set itself, spartan in the extreme, emphasising the musicians onstage, all semblance of extraneous equipment hidden from view, a feature of Yes shows until the mid-1990s. Split screen is used to very good effect, however, allowing the viewer access to multiple views, an aspect which has worn rather better.

On the second American leg of the *90125* tour, after their European dates across the summer, the band were clearly well-drilled and full of energy. Opening with 'Cinema' and going into 'Leave It', complete with vocal enhancements, the band really show their skill with 'Hold On' before a searing 'I've Seen All Good People', which Rabin really makes his own. The stock footage here has – unsurprisingly – people turning their heads.

A precise 'Changes' is followed by an exuberant, extended 'Make It Easy'/'Owner', then 'It Can Happen', which has embellishments from Anderson at the end that feel almost like gospel. 'City Of Love' is suitably menacing with a showcase for Rabin and then it's straight into 'Starship Trooper' and the credits. The video was nominated for a Grammy for Best Longform Music Video.

The 2006 DVD contains a version of 'Roundabout', some backstage band footage and a director's cut version that cuts out some – but not all – of the added video footage.

Various bootlegs exist of the entire shows, of course, and some TV footage was shot on video (and so feels quite different, as well as presenting the audio in a slightly rawer form) in Dortmund,

Germany, during the European leg in June. The band are in similar stage clothes, except Rabin, who is sporting a striking red jacket.

To accompany the 1985 video was a live album: *9012live The Solos*. While it clearly made sense to release this from a marketing point of view to accompany the video, this one stands out as something of a folly. Although two live tracks are featured – 'Hold On' and 'Changes', from the soundtrack to the video – while a 2009 reissue also adds 'City Of Love' and 'It Can Happen', the rest of the album is very much 'play it once' fodder, containing as it does the solo spots from each of the artists. It's well done, but hardly essential listening. Kaye's solo 'Si' contains some powerful church organ and a snippet of Bach's 'Toccata', while Rabin's 'Solly's Beard' accompanied by Kaye, is flashy but doesn't come across well on record. Anderson gives us 'Soon' from *Relayer*, again with Kaye accompanying, a well-received exercise in nostalgia rather than something with much merit as a listen. The rest of the album (11 minutes, if we're counting) is given over to Squire and White, firstly with the bassist's eardrum-bursting bass pedal rendition of 'Amazing Grace', which he'd also played on the *Drama* tour. They then launch into 'Whitefish', which starts with 'The Fish', before instrumental renditions of 'Tempus Fugit' from *Drama* and 'Sound Chaser' from *Relayer*.

Even with the addition of the bonus tracks and 'Roundabout' on the DVD, this still leaves the following songs that were played regularly on the tour unaccounted for: 'Hearts', 'Our Song', 'Yours Is No Disgrace', 'Long Distance Runaround' and 'And You And I'. A full live document would have been wonderful, given the sheer energy and joy the band were putting out at the time. Let's hope something can be found some time – perhaps for Record Store Day. The live shows really deserve it.

What *9012live The Solos* does do, however, is emphasise the sheer number of people – many of them new members of the team – that went into the creation of such a massive tour. It's notable that South African Paul DeVilliers was the live sound engineer, and the lighting engineer was Merle McLain, so no roles for Nigel Luby and Michael Tait, both of whom had been crucial parts of the Yes team for over ten years.

Mickey Heyes, assistant tour manager, said this of the tour on the sleeve notes to the live album:

> Aside from seeing three continents, three tour managers, one small army of Argentinian security, encountering numerous threats, one

> ticket office bombing, some minor bickering and moaning, one squadron of flying saucers over Denver, lots of vodka and surviving two international escapes, the tour went smoothly and without incident.

The mind boggles. But it was the 1980s.

90125 – Played Live Over The Years

Thanks to forgotten-yesterdays.com for the number of plays for each song. Figures include Yes and ARW but not ABWH, Anderson solo, Rabin solo or other Yes-linked performances, such as The Trevor Horn Band

Three songs from *90125* failed to survive the tour and live on beyond the end of the album's natural cycle, somewhat better than the less-favoured *Big Generator*, where 'Rhythm Of Love' was the only song to make it to the *Talk* tour (for instance). As with many Yes songs from all eras, the pieces on the album were tightly arranged, with only limited possibilities for re-arrangement and extension, but there have been little tweaks over the years. The songs have also suffered from the stark division between Rabin and Howe versions of the band, and even on the *Union* tour, Howe didn't play on the Rabin songs.

So, unlike 'And You And I' or 'Perpetual Change' (just to give two examples), most of the pieces have not crossed over, although Howe has – somewhat reluctantly – played 'Owner' in various arrangements, and with Sherwood a full member of the band, 'Cinema' and 'Hearts' came back into the set.

'Owner Of A Lonely Heart' Played 1092 Times

The band's biggest hit is the sixth most played song in the Yes canon behind 'Roundabout', 'And You And I', 'I've Seen All Good People', 'Starship Trooper' and 'Heart Of The Sunrise'. Not surprisingly, it has been played throughout the band's history, most recently by ARW in 2018. When played by Rabin versions of the band, it has almost always been introduced by Rabin's 'Make It Easy' (in instrumental form – played 437 times). It was performed in such a way throughout the *90125*, *Big Generator*, *Union*, *Talk* and ARW tours. However, with Billy Sherwood in the band as a more-than-adequate Rabin replacement, bands with Howe in were able to play the song without him needing to be involved, as they did in 1998, 1999 and 2000. Sherwood told me:

> I covered the Rabin guitar parts, as Steve wasn't interested in that. That role fell into my lap by proxy. I wasn't looking to be the lead guitar player in Yes. But I loved playing those parts – we did 'Hearts' as well – so I took all the main solos and interpreted them in my own way.

Later, Howe (somewhat reluctantly) played the song himself as one of only three concessions to the Rabin era, the other two being 'Rhythm Of Love', which he played on the 2004 world tour with some enthusiasm and, as mentioned by Sherwood, 'Hearts' in 1999 and 2000. As the connection between the current band and the *90125* era faded following Squire's passing in 2015, 'Owner' was finally dropped and hasn't been played regularly by the Howe version of the band since 2016.

As for the arrangement, it generally stayed fairly close to the original, perhaps with a little more freedom and exuberance than originally envisaged by Horn. However, the closing section is a good opportunity for expansion and soloing, and this has been a regular occurrence. The *Union* tour, for instance, saw the *90125* five-piece play the song, but then Wakeman would return to the stage for a searing Minimoog solo. On the ARW tour, Rabin and Wakeman took this one step further, going walkabout in whatever venue they were playing in while both musicians soloed – Wakeman with a keytar (a strap-on synthesiser). On *The Ladder* tour, the song was played with Sherwood playing the lead parts but with a solo in the extended outro from Steve Howe.

The most radical reworking by the full band was on the 2004 world tour, which saw the band perform the song as part of the acoustic set at the start of the second half, as seen on the *Song From Tsongas* DVD. Howe plays his parts well, although he sits with something of a stoney face, and the solo is a jaunty piano break from Rick Wakeman.

The song was played in 2017 when Yes were inducted into the Rock and Roll Hall of Fame and in 2022 at the Alan White tribute concert in Seattle.

The question remains: will Yes ever play it again? It's possible that they might, but as every year goes by, it looks less and less likely. Will Anderson ever play it again? I'm certain of it. He's probably playing it tonight somewhere.

'Hold On' Played 343 Times

Another favourite of the Rabin era, 'Hold On' was played throughout the *90125* and *Big Generator* tours. It was also played on some – but not all – of the *Talk* tour dates and performed once in a while on the *Union* tour in 1991. ARW also played it throughout 2016, 2017 and 2018. Although it can be extended slightly, it is normally played roughly in the same arrangement as the album version.

'It Can Happen' Played 114 times
The album's third single never made it beyond the *90125* tour, perhaps surprisingly.

'Changes' Played 417 times
Perhaps underlining its status as a Yes classic, 'Changes' was pretty much the first song to be picked for the set whenever Rabin was in the band. It was played throughout the *90125*, *Big Generator*, *Union*, *Talk* and ARW tours at every concert.

Played pretty straight in 1984 and 1985, it has undergone a few arrangement embellishments over the years while sticking to the established song structure. On the *Talk* tour, the instrumental introduction was extended for extra tension and a little opportunity for Squire to show off, as did Rabin in his super-fast solo, which was also extended by a few bars. With Anderson taking a breather until the 'one word from you' section, both Rabin and Sherwood sang on the first iteration of the chorus with Squire, which sounded … odd. But actually, in a tight 150-minute set with no formal solo sections, it's important to give each musician little breaks, and this was Anderson's.

'Cinema' played 335 times
The short instrumental is almost always used as some sort of introduction – either to the whole concert or to herald the encores – as it was on *The Ladder* tour, with guitar parts played by Billy Sherwood. It was used throughout the *90125*, *Talk* and ARW tours, but surprisingly not on the *Big Generator* tour. It either introduces 'Leave It', as it did on the *90125* tour, 'Owner' as part of a short *90125* section on *The Ladder* tour or the entire concert, as it did with ARW.

'Leave It' played 114 times
Performed with White on electronic drums and using Casey Young to enhance the vocals, it's hardly surprising that 'Leave It' failed to make it past the *90125* tour despite its minor hit single status.

'Our Song' played 36 times
Given that an early version of this song must have been played many times in rehearsals, it's a shame that this gem was played so few times on the *90125* tour and never since. Played early on the tour, it was revived for the late summer and early autumn shows in the US in 1984. And that's it.

'City Of Love' played 155 times

Given that this song is easily extended and gives the opportunity for some showmanship in various areas, it's hardly surprising that it's featured a little more in the set, played during the *90125* and *Talk* tours in an arrangement that allowed an extended solo for Rabin. It also made a single appearance on the *Union* tour.

'Hearts' played 250 times

Like 'City Of Love', 'Hearts' was played throughout the *90125* and *Talk* tours with an additional full-band section before Kaye's familiar synth introduction. Indeed, the version recorded in Santiago in Chile on YouTube, towards the end of the *Talk* tour, shows what an asset Kaye was to the band as a performer, relishing every moment of his Hammond solo.

But the song was also dusted off for *The Ladder* tour, with Billy Sherwood interpreting Rabin's solos, Igor Khoroshev as Tony Kaye and additional pedal steel from Steve Howe. Sadly, this song failed to make the cut for the *House Of Blues* live DVD, which is a shame.

What Happened Next?

The band came back from a year of touring. They had been treated like royalty, they had played to huge, enthusiastic audiences every night, including a lot of new fans. Kaye sums up that time:

> I can honestly say that the band were on top of the world at that point. It was slightly dysfunctional – but aren't all bands. Everyone was having a great time, making money and flying around on a private jet, playing huge shows every night. It was fun! It was all good memories – looking back all these years later, it was a good time. The band were playing very well. Alan was on top of his game; Chris was playing amazingly. Success brings enthusiasm, and it brings out the happiness of playing every night. Even Jon was happy!

But then the band had to follow it up, and it wasn't so easy. Rabin sketches out the problem the band had:

> When an album comes out and it's so successful and the process of making it has been so peculiar, you then realise that you have a bunch of guys that have never really worked together apart from being on stage. I didn't really know Jon at all, but by this stage, Chris was like a brother to me, and it continued that way after I left the band. I loved Alan and Tony, too. For the next album, the record company – who had no idea what had gone down during the recording of *90125* – suggested Trevor Horn again. Tony said, 'No way', and it became clear that Trevor was going to do it, but he wasn't going to work with Tony. Trevor wanted me to do most of the keyboards again.
>
> We had an offer to do the album at a castle in Italy, and I thought that was a good idea. Unfortunately, it was a bit of a party period, so very little was achieved. In terms of writing together, there was no cohesiveness whatsoever and the atmosphere between certain people was very toxic.
>
> I have to say that, on stage, Tony Kaye was just perfect for the band. He couldn't have been better. But at one point during *Big Generator*, he was in one room working on something while I was in another room working on the keyboards as well. After their experience on *90125*, the bad blood was there from the start. Trevor and I would listen to his parts, and I wouldn't necessarily like what I was hearing, but I would be diplomatic because I didn't want to be 'anti-Tony'. It was all very delicate.

The band moved back to London to continue recording for a while, and then Horn left the project, with the band ending up in Los Angeles, where Rabin took responsibility.

> To cut a long story short, a friend of mine from South Africa, Paul De Villiers, came in to help finish the recording in California, and in the end, I went into Sunset Sound in LA and said, 'Just leave me alone, and let me finish it.' It was the only option we had to get a finished album. But I really enjoyed working on the album on my own. There was some disillusionment after *Big Generator*, where I'd been a salvage producer, if anything.

The new album was released in September 1987, some two years after recording had first started in Italy. Two singles reached the top 40 in the US – 'Rhythm Of Love' and 'Love Will Find A Way' – but neither reached the heights of 'Owner', and the album itself, despite platinum certification in the US, failed to sell anything like its predecessor worldwide. A tour of the US and Japan (but, tellingly, not Europe) ended in April 1988, at which point Anderson left once again, frustrated by the direction of the band and his lack of influence.

The band were rudderless for a while. Rabin recorded *Can't Look Away*, an excellent solo album produced (ironically) by Bob Ezrin, which did well but failed to launch him as a bestselling solo artist. He also did some writing with Supertramp's Roger Hodgson. Meanwhile, Anderson continued his solo career with a decent solo album, *In The City Of Angels*. Squire began to work with a young chap called Billy Sherwood of World Trade, who was also touted (somewhat against his will) as a new vocalist in Yes.

The story behind the Anderson, Bruford, Wakeman, Howe and *Union* periods is best left for another book, but managerial manoeuvring brought together ABWH and 'Yes West', as the remaining Rabin/Kaye lineup was nicknamed, for the bodged *Union* album (albeit with some excellent moments, most of which were provided by Yes West).

When the eight-man behemoth splintered after that hugely successful world tour, the band were offered a deal with Phil Carson's new Victory label, owned by Japanese conglomerate JVC. Carson wanted commercial success and instinctively felt that the *90125* lineup would produce that. This time, however, there would be no Horn, and Trevor Rabin was tasked with pulling the album together. Again, there were to be twists and turns aplenty during this period, not least

Rabin's decision to record the album to hard disc during the infancy of such technology. Although Anderson was far better integrated into the writing process this time, it remains very much Rabin's album. It's a mixture of song-orientated Yes material with Rabin's flair for guitar orchestration. The band took the album on a lengthy tour, incorporating North America, South America and Japan, but the failure of Victory Records, alongside the relatively poor performance of the album itself, led to modest ticket sales for the tour. Although the band played superbly, helped by guest musician Billy Sherwood on vocals, guitar, keyboards and – thrillingly – bass during the epic 'Endless Dream', someone had to carry the can, and in the end, it was Rabin.

For both Rabin and Kaye, it was the end of the road as members of Yes. 'Things started to get a little dark,' Kaye remembers. 'I was pretty fed up with touring and I felt it was the end of the road.' Rabin concurs. 'After the tour, I felt I was persona non-grata. I took responsibility for the commercial failure of *Talk*, and I had to live with it. But that spurred on my move into film music.'

For Rabin and Kaye, this would be their last formal involvement in Yes full stop, but both members would find their membership difficult to shake off completely as the band itself continued in various different incarnations. Kaye carried on with his life in Los Angeles for many years before moving to the West Coast of Florida. He reappeared with the band during the 50th-anniversary celebrations in the US and that also saw Patrick Moraz perform occasionally.

Rabin moved into film and TV work for many years, but in 2016, he accepted an invitation to form a touring band with Jon Anderson and Rick Wakeman (with whom he had struck up a firm friendship) in a band called Anderson, Rabin, Wakeman, later renamed (inadvisedly, perhaps) Yes, featuring Anderson, Rabin, Wakeman. The trio – with a guest rhythm section – toured for nearly two years off and on, playing a choice mixture of 1970s and 1980s material, including 'Cinema', 'Owner', 'Hold On' and 'Changes' from *90125*. Surprisingly, 'Hearts' failed to make an appearance. When new material failed to materialise, barring a lovely song 'Fragile', whose only official release was as a bonus track on Rabin's 2023 solo album *Rio*, the project disbanded.

Yes Post Rabin And Kaye

But Yes continued, as the band still does in 2024. As I write this, I will be seeing them later this evening in Bristol on their *Tales Of Classic Yes* tour.

A change of management and approach in 1995 saw Steve Howe and later Rick Wakeman rejoin for some concerts in Anderson's then-hometown of San Louis Obispo in California. The *Keys To Ascension* albums are considered by some to be misguided, mixing live versions of Yes classics with some more than decent studio material, including two long-form pieces: 'That That Is' and 'Mind Drive'. Although the studio tracks were later gathered together in one album, it felt incomplete, and by the time volume two was released, there was another Yes. Opportunistically, Anderson, Howe and White had become involved in a project that Chris Squire and Billy Sherwood had been working on, which became the *Open Your Eyes* album and tour, with Sherwood reprising his role as a very useful jack of all trades and the talented Igor Khoroshev on keyboards. This band then made a properly collaborative album in *The Ladder* and toured that album as well.

Despite Steve Howe's understandable reluctance to play Rabin-era material, the presence of Billy Sherwood allowed the band to keep 'Cinema', 'Owner' and even 'Hearts' in the set, even though Sherwood would be the first to admit that he lacked the virtuosity of Rabin as a lead guitarist.

Sherwood moved on in 2000, as did Khoroshev – the latter after the *Masterworks* tour under something of a cloud – leaving Yes without a keyboard player. Therefore, they recorded the next album *Magnification* – released in 2001 – with an orchestra instead and Alan White providing the odd flourish of piano. Released the same week as 9/11, the album was a flop, but the tour – featuring a live orchestra every night – was something of a triumph. Wakeman was back for the next few years, which included 35th anniversary celebrations in 2002, 2003 and 2004. The latter tour saw a return to arenas and a long, career-spanning set, including an acoustic interlude. In truth, those two years were probably too gruelling for musicians in their mid to late 50s, and after that, the band went on hiatus.

The Ladder tour of 1999 and 2000 had been the last time that the band had really 'toured' an album, and from that enforced hiatus onwards, Yes entered a difficult period. Firstly, Wakeman – who had been in and out of the band for almost 40 years – decided not to tour as extensively as he previously had and gave up his position to his eldest son Oliver – very much a chip off the old block. Secondly, Anderson suffered a fall in which he damaged his back and then later suffered a major respiratory failure, meaning he could not tour – as it turned out – for a couple of years.

The decision that the remaining members took changed the path of the band and resonates with many fans today. Anderson was out, replaced by another singer, the amiable French-Canadian Benoit David. This lineup toured for a couple of years, but when Trevor Horn took over production for the *Fly From Here* album in 2011, Oliver was out, replaced by Horn's fellow Buggle and comrade of Steve Howe in Asia, Geoff Downes. When Benoit suffered voice problems, he, too, was replaced by Jon Davison, and that lineup recorded the undercooked *Heaven And Earth* album in 2013. Meanwhile, the band continued to tour, playing 'album series' shows, incorporating *The Yes Album, Fragile, Close To The Edge, Going For The One* and even *Drama*.

The last two lineup changes were brought about under tragic circumstances. Chris Squire succumbed to cancer in 2015, having passed his bass position on to a returning Billy Sherwood. Furthermore, Alan White – having suffered ill health for some years, meaning that he was more of a talisman at live shows than an active participant – also passed away in 2022, replaced by his long-time stand-in, American Jay Schellen. The band were incorporated into the Rock And Roll Hall Of Fame in 2017 at an uncomfortable show which saw Rabin and Howe onstage together for the first time since 1992, playing 'Owner' (with Howe on bass) and 'Roundabout' (with Geddy Lee of Rush on bass). The 50th anniversary celebrations in 2018 saw Moraz and Kaye participate in the US and Bill Bruford introduced the band in London. This lineup, with Howe at the helm, have recorded two well-received albums – *The Quest* and *Mirror To The Sky* – and while a few songs from these records have been played live, the band now seem content to play variations of greatest hits sets to theatre-size audiences, with the occasional larger show.

Meanwhile, Anderson has stayed active into his late 70s, touring with The Paul Green Rock Academy and The Band Geeks, playing Yes classics, as he is entitled to do. Kaye released a debut solo album *The End Of Innocence* in 2021, and after a long career recording soundtracks, Rabin recorded the excellent and varied solo album *Rio* in 2023.

Conclusion

But did *90125* save Yes? What if Anderson hadn't returned and the album had been released as Cinema? Rabin has always felt that it would have done well anyway without the band being called Yes. But would it? Carson believes that 'Owner' was good enough to be a hit without Anderson, but a record deal was far from certain until the very last minute. In fact, Carson is the unsung hero of *90125*, bankrolling Cinema personally for many months. Although Anderson's solo career at that point had hardly set the charts alight, his work with Vangelis had produced two hit albums and two big hit singles in 'I Hear You Now' and 'I'll Find My Way Home'. Anderson was a commercial bet, not just because he was the previous lead vocalist of Yes but because he was still in the public eye. Nonetheless, there's little doubt that the fairy dust he sprinkled over the album enhanced it creatively as well as commercially.

90125 went through a unique writing, rehearsal and recording process that makes it unlike most albums. Rabin maintains rightly that '*90125* mainly comes from my garage in LA. A few songs we hadn't rehearsed initially but we brought in later, like 'Changes'. And some of the newer stuff we tacked onto other parts that we had rehearsed at John Henry's'. The first phase saw Rabin demo his material in California while White and Squire rehearsed with Page, building a smaller stock of material to use. Next, the Cinema foursome developed and refined that material at the rehearsal studio in London during most of 1982. Phase three saw the album recorded with Horn, during which the best material was chosen, and the last phase saw Cinema become Yes, with Anderson's astonishing return.

But would Yes have continued at some point anyway? Like many of the bands from the 1970s, they might well have reformed eventually. But it's also very likely that the success of *90125* and the extra fans its success gave the band, many of whom went back and discovered the joys of the earlier material, injected a shot in the arm that remains in the band's immune system today.

Rick Wakeman has no doubt about what the album did for the band in terms of longevity:

> I think that was the most important area because if that hadn't happened, there wouldn't be a Yes today. I can understand why Yes fans don't like it because it and *Big Generator* are in a completely different genre, but it gave the band a massive boost and kept it alive.

Despite the very 1980s production techniques and a certain antipathy, even snobbery, amongst some fans of the 1970s era towards this 1980s version of Yes in general, the album has aged remarkably well. Like all the best music from that colourful decade, it is the material that ensures its longevity. There is not one poor track on the album, and the way it's sequenced makes it a wonderful one-sitting listen.

In *Adventures In Modern Recoding*, Trevor Horn sums up his feelings about the album:

> They remain my favourite group, and I'm happy to say that even if I don't think *90125* is the best Yes album – that honour would have to go to *Close To The Edge* or maybe *Relayer* – it is their best-selling.

And of 'Owner' itself?

> I think that, in retrospect, it was worth it, whatever shit it put me through.

90125 looms large to this day, including with members of the current version of the band, even if the current configuration of Yes doesn't allow material from the era to be played. Billy Sherwood told me how he found the impetus to play that material when he got the chance:

> But it all boils down to holding that music in my heart, and the passion I felt for it allowed me to do that.

Strong emotions indeed. Clearly, for Sherwood, as well as many others, including your author, *90125* is not a contrived and cynical 1980s recording that the band got away with (as some would argue). It's a superb album. One of the best of the 1980s.

History often repeats itself, and Yes, as a band, are prone to highs and lows – often within a few years or even months. But for almost everyone concerned, it seems to have been a happy time. So, we'll give the final word to Trevor Rabin. This was a period in his life that he, in particular, remembers very fondly:

> To this day, I really miss Chris and Alan – the three-piece juggernaut, as I used to call us. I just loved playing with them.

Bibliography And Other Sources

Much of the content of this book was taken from interviews with its protagonists:

Jon Anderson (2023), Trevor Rabin (2023 and 2024), Phil Carson (2023), Billy Sherwood (2024) and Tony Kaye (2024)

Horn, T. *Adventures In Modern Recording* (Nine Eight Books, 2022)
Welch, C., *Close To The Edge – The Story Of Yes* (Omnibus Press, 1998)
Popoff, M., *Time And A Word – The Yes Story* (Soundcheck Books, 2016)
Watkinson, D., *Yes – Perpetual Change* (Plexus, 2001)
Romano, W., *Close To The Edge* (Backbeat, 2017)
O'Reilly, S., *Yes And Philosophy* (Self Published, 2012)
Morse, T., *Yes Stories – Yes In Their Own Words* (St. Martin's Griffin, 1996)
Chambers, S., *Yes – An Endless Dream Of '70s, '80s And '90s Rock Music* (General Store, 2002)
Farley, A., *The Extraordinary World Of Yes* (iUniverse Inc, 2004)
Kirkman, J. *Dialogue – The Yes Interviews* (Classic Rock Vaults Books, 2019)
Lambe, S. with Watkinson, D., *Yes In The 1980s* (Sonicbond Publishing, 2021)
Lambe, S. *Yes On Track* (Sonicbond Publishing, 2018 and 2023)
Mulryne, K., *Yes. The Tormato Story* (Self Published, 2023)
Barrow, S. *Solid Mental Grace – Listening To The Music Of Yes* (Cultured Lama, 2018)
Howe, S. *All My Yesterdays* (Omnibus, 2020)
Lee, G. *My Effin' Life* (Harper, 2023)
Power, M. *No Quarter: The Three Lives Of Jimmy Page* (Omnibus, 2016)
Blake, M. *Us And Them: The Authorised Story Of Hipgnosis* (Nine Eight Books, 2023)
Bassols, Gerard. *The Musical Instruments Of Progressive Rock* (Circulo Rojo, 2019)

Some quotes were taken from *Yes: Classic Rock Artists* DVD (Black Hill)
Notes From The Edge #270. Interview with Trevor Rabin by Mike Tiano

Loudersound.com Interview with Gary Mouat, 2015
Rock Candy magazine interview with Trevor Rabin, Issue 83, December 2020
The quotes from Casey Young and the memories of Jon Dee were taken from *www.yesmusicpodcast.com*
Eddie Jobson's comments were taken from *Yesfans.com*

Online resources

yesworld.com – the official Yes website
yesfans.com – long-running fan site and forum
yesmusicpodcast.com – excellent weekly podcast about the band
bondegezou.co.uk – website of long-term Yes chronicler Henry Potts
forgotten-yesterdays.com – invaluable online resource
setlist.fm – invaluable archive of setlists

Facebook has many Yes-related groups. Join them at your leisure (or, indeed, peril).

Also available from Sonicbond Publishing

The Rock Classics Series

90125 by Yes – Stephen Lambe
978-1-78952-329-4

Bat Out Of Hell by Meatloaf – Geoffrey Feakes
978-1-78952-320-1

Bringing It All Back Home by Bob Dylan – Opher Goodwin
978-1-78952-314-0

Californication by The Red Hot Chili Peppers – Matt Karpe
978-1-78952-348-5

Crime Of The Century by Supertramp – Steve Pilkington
978-1-78952-327-0

The Dreaming by Kate Bush – Peter Kearns
978-1-78952-341-6

Let It Bleed by The Rolling Stones – John Van der Kiste
978-1-78952-309-6

Purple Rain by Prince – Matt Karpe
978-1-78952-327-0

The White Album by The Beatles – Opher Goodwin
978-1-78952-333-1

Who's Next by The Who – Ian Sharp
978-1-78952-345-4

Would you like to write for Sonicbond Publishing?

We are mainly a music publisher, but we also occasionally publish in other genres including film and television. At Sonicbond Publishing we are always on the look-out for authors, particularly for our two main series, On Track and Decades.

Mixing fact with in depth analysis, the On Track series examines the entire recorded work of a particular musical artist or group. All genres are considered from easy listening and jazz to 60s soul to 90s pop, via rock and metal.

The Decades series singles out a particular decade in an artist or group's history and focuses on that decade in more detail than may be allowed in the On Track series.

While professional writing experience would, of course, be an advantage, the most important qualification is to have real enthusiasm and knowledge of your subject. First-time authors are welcomed, but the ability to write well in English is essential.

Sonicbond Publishing has distribution throughout Europe and North America, and all our books are also published in E-book form. Authors will be paid a royalty based on sales of their book.

Further details about our books are available from www.sonicbondpublishing.com. To contact us, complete the contact form there or email info@sonicbondpublishing.co.uk